BREAD FROM HEAVEN
Trusting God To Become Debt Free

BREAD FROM HEAVEN
Trusting God To Become Debt Free

DAISY S. DANIELS

THE WRITING ON THE WALL PUBLISHING SERVICES
ORLANDO, FL 32862, U.S.A.

BREAD FROM HEAVEN: Trusting God To Become Debt Free
Daisy S. Daniels
P.O. Box 621433
Orlando, Florida 32862 – 1433
Website:
www.thewritingonthewal.wix.com/daisysdaniels
E-Mail address: thewritingonthewall@aol.com

Library of Congress Control Number: 2015908503

ISBN 978-0-9914002-3-2

Table of Content

Introduction
In Eleven Days

I couldn't get in the Lord's presence fast enough before He started ministering to me. Immediately the vision was before me:

In a vision...

I saw my daughter's dog, Kane (a boy, white, pit bull, who my daughter endearingly calls her baby) looking up at me. Then I see Sugar (my daughter's other baby, a girl, white, pit bull, identical to her brother Kane), sneaking under the table and resting her head on my lap.

Immediately I was overcome with the fear that I felt the first time I met them: My husband, Randolph, and I arrived at my daughter's house. As we stood in the garage, she explained what was about to happen. "When you go in your room, close the door. They're going to come to the door and sniff under the door; to get your scent, so they'll know who's in the house. After that, they'll go back into their room."

"But wait!" I said anxiously. "Where are they now?"

"They're in my room. You don't have to worry, they can't get out."

"Oh, my gosh! Where is your room compared to the room we'll be in?"

"It's a few feet away. You'll have to pass my room in order to get to your ro…"

"DaiSha! Nooo!" I interrupted.

"Don't worry, Mom! It's okay. Just go in the room and close the door."

"But DaiSha! Oh, my gosh! I don't know if I'm ready. We have to go pass the room where they are? Is there any other way we can do this?"

"No, Mom. And since you're here from Florida, I don't think you have another option."

"Help me, Jesus!" I said as the thought of just tip-toeing past the room they were in proved not to be an option either. As soon as we went into the house, you could hear them upstairs anxiously waiting to get out of the room. There was no doubt; they knew somebody else had come in the house other than "mom." We quickly ran into the room and not only did I close the door, but I locked it. With my feet planted, I stood with my hands against the door to keep the dogs out (in case the lock on the door failed). I was terrified.

And seemingly, as soon as I locked the door, there was a big BOOM! against the door, as the dogs came running out of the room to see who was in their house. Then there was a huge sniff under the door. And I mean, with everything that this dog had in him, he took the deepest, longest, sniff I'd ever heard! I kid you not! I was sure everything that was in the room: bed, TV, dresser, Randolph, and I were getting ready to go under the door as the dog took in the scent of the strangers in his house. I was praying, "Please, Lord. Help us, Jesus!" I was terrified. And just as suddenly as the vision appeared, the tears started to roll down my face as I realized the interpretation of the vision:

I was afraid.

But the vision revealed this time I wasn't afraid of Kane and Sugar, but afraid of what the Lord was telling me to do. I was terrified. Yet again, I would be exposed. My deepest secrets, private struggles, and personal battles were about to be exposed. And as if to answer my concern, another vision was before me:

I saw one of the Twin Towers with a cloud of black smoke surrounding it, suddenly collapse. Then the second tower was before me, it too had a cloud of black smoke surrounding it, but it was still standing. And the Lord said, "You refuse to fall."

The tears continued to roll down my face, and the tissues started to pile up. The Lord said, *"Your system doesn't work."* And immediately I was reminded of, yes, 9/11. For hundreds of thousands, millions of Americans, 9/11 marked the start of a lifelong, downward spiral of life as we *knew* it. For those who lost loved ones, who are forever mourned, my deepest condolences. To those who survived, but are forever impacted, my prayers go out to you.

For the rest of us, 9/11 is a reflection of not only a terrorist attack, but an attack on the financial well-being of the United States of America. It wasn't an attack on the "Twin Towers," as much as it was an attack on what they represented. As the stock markets crashed, banks, and other financial institutions quickly scrambled to keep their heads above water.

However, their resilience proved to be a little more difficult to do when the "housing market" collapsed. And we, America, found ourselves on the verge of the economy completely collapsing; causing us to come as close to a "great depression" as we could come without getting there.

Again, I couldn't help but be reminded of the hundreds of thousands, millions of Americans who were, and *still* are, trying to recover years later. In fact, I realize there are hundreds of thousands, millions of Americans who may not *ever* recover.

"Your system doesn't work," I was reminded.

The rich rule over the poor,
and the borrower is slave to the lender.

Proverbs 22:7 NIV

Most of us don't realize debt is a form of bondage. It's a form of oppression. While we've become accustomed to living on credit, we've overlooked the fact that by doing so, we've become slaves to the lender. Because we've entered into an agreement to borrow, whether it's a financial loan or credit, we are subject to the lender; their terms. And by doing so, we become obligated to repay the debt.

Therefore, the lender; whether an individual or a financial institution, dictates to us what we are able to do with our money. And as long as we're in that agreement, we're their servants; they are our masters. And consequently, we no longer have the freedom to do with our money what we choose; until the debt is paid of course.

Now, don't get me wrong, this is not to say that we can't ever have credit, but it is to say that we should consider very carefully and wisely who we go into debt with, why we're going into debt, and are we *really* able to honor the agreement that we've entered into; because until the debt is satisfied, we're a slave to the lender. We have to use wisdom; count up the cost.

So often we find ourselves overextended – all of our money spent, our credit maxed out, and on the verge of, if not already, bankruptcy. And now we've found ourselves in a situation that we don't know how to get out of: foolishly spending all of our money on things that have no value; things that only give momentary pleasures; things to try to "keep up with the Jones," which have also proven to be our own undoing.

We live beyond our means.

As I sat in the Lord's presence, the vision was before me:

I saw a single cluster of Grapes.

As I continued to sit before the Lord to receive the interpretation, in my spirit I understood grapes represent wealth. So, I waited for the Lord to reveal to me what He was saying.

When they came to the valley of Eshcol, they cut down a branch with <u>a single cluster of grapes</u> so large that it took two of them to carry it on a pole between them!

Numbers 13:23a NLT (emphasis added)

Immediately, I got excited! Needless to say, I knew the grapes had come from the Promised Land. And God was not only revealing the abundance that's in the Promised Land, but He was getting ready to take us into the Promised Land.

Well, let me go back a little bit, so that you may be excited as well.

In Numbers, chapter thirteen, it talks about the twelve scouts or the twelve spies that went to explore Canaan:

The LORD now said to Moses,

"Send out men <u>to explore</u> the land of Canaan, the land I am giving to the Israelites.

Numbers 13:1-2a NLT (emphasis added)

Moses gave the men these instructions as he sent them out to explore the land: "...Do your best to bring back samples of the crops you see."

(It happened to be the season for harvesting the first ripe grapes.)

Numbers 13:17a; 20c NLT

So it was clear; before the children of Israel were allowed to enter into the Promised Land, they had to first "explore" the land to see what they were up against. To "explore" means to examine it carefully; investigate. And it's understood that *before* we're able to possess the land, we have to examine it carefully; we have to investigate the land carefully to see what's in the land.

Then, I have to say, my immediate thought was *what do I need to know about possessing the Promised Land before I'm able to possess it? What do I need to examine carefully in order to possess the land? What do I need to investigate before I'm able to possess the land?* My questions seemed to reveal my own self-examination. I also understood that *I* was being examined carefully, investigated before being able to enter into the Promised Land.

It *"happened to be"* the season for harvesting the first ripe grapes? *It didn't happen to be* – I knew the Lord was revealing – *it was my season!* It was time to receive the *first harvest* of the seeds that I had sown. It was time for me to receive the abundance that the Lord has for me. I knew it was going to be huge based on the size of the grapes! Huge! And it was going to take more than just me to bring in the harvest; a single cluster of grapes! Huge!

"But you all came to me and said, 'First, let's send out scouts to explore the land for us. They will advise us on the best route to take and which towns we should enter.'

Deuteronomy 1:22 NLT

Guess what? They had a plan before they just entered into the Promised Land. The plan was to find out the best route to take and which towns they should enter. And immediately, I asked, "Lord, what's the best route to take and how do we get there?"

I wanted to know what the Lord was doing and prayed that He would reveal His plan to me, so that I may be careful to follow His direction, His instructions as He leads me. I was ready to possess the land. As I continued to sit in the Lord's presence, I realized the spies had to be skilled in order to go into the land and examine it; they had to be skilled in order to be able to "bring back the report."

And suddenly, I started to see the connection in the Lord being concerned about us being in debt and us going into the Promised Land. It made sense. How are we going to go into the Promised Land that's flowing with milk and honey – in debt? How are we going to receive the Lord's abundance if we're in debt? Burdened? Oppressed?

"They picked some of its fruit and brought it back to us. And they reported, 'The land the LORD our God has given us is indeed a good land.'

Deuteronomy 1:25 NLT

I couldn't help but be reminded that what should've only taken eleven days took the children of Israel forty years:

Normally it takes only eleven days to travel from Mount Sinai to Kadesh-barnea, going by way of Mount Seir.

Deuteronomy 1:2 NLT

So, as I sat before the Lord, in my spirit I believed the Lord was getting ready to do *something* "in eleven days." In eleven days I was getting ready to enter into the Promised Land (because unlike the children of Israel, I believed the Lord). I trusted the Lord with everything that I have.

So I stood on the word of the Lord and declared, "In eleven days, I shall enter into the Promised Land!"

One
Bread from Heaven

As the man of God ministered, he said, "God is going to give you bread from heaven."

Immediately, I received *the word* in my spirit. I was expecting the Lord to show up and do something *miraculous* in my life as I stood on His word. In eleven days!

Then the LORD said to Moses, "I will rain down bread from heaven for you. The people are to go out each day and gather enough for that day. In this way I will test them to see whether they will follow my instructions.

Exodus 16:4 NIV

A promise: to provide, for His people.

I wanted His promise. I wanted Him to provide for me supernaturally.

And yet, as He gives His promise, He makes known that there are specific instructions that we must follow in order to obtain the promise. By this, He will test us to see if we will follow His instructions.

While many of us are definitely *ready and waiting* for the Lord's promises to manifest in our lives, we have yet to pass the test by following His instructions. Are you wondering why you're not seeing the manifested blessings in your life? Are you wondering why the Lord hasn't blessed you as of yet? Well, let me ask you this, are you following the Lord's instructions?

Yes, the Lord said He'll bless us. Yes, He said He'll provide for us, but He also said that we have to follow His instructions, His commands in order to receive the blessings. Let me see if I can make this plain for you. There is only one thing that results in the blessings and that is – obedience.

Let's start here: ***The people are to go out each day and gather enough for that day.*** The Lord said that He'll provide for you enough for that day. Everything that you need for today, He has already provided. He has already given you. Not for tomorrow. For today! Right now! What do you need for right now? And I hope you know that this doesn't, by any chance, mean that you won't live in abundance, that you won't live in the land of more than enough. But it does mean by this, He'll test you to see if you'll follow His instructions.

I can't help but be reminded of a time when I was getting ready to have a women's conference, and I was looking for a place to have the conference. After many phone calls, leaving message after message, days of waiting for someone to return my call, only to be advised of costs that exceeded my budget. Then, I was excited and jumped at the offer that came closest to my budget and met my accommodations. The Lord had made a way!

Now after a few days or so, I was having trouble getting the signed contract to the sales manager; I was faxing it but she wasn't getting it. In the mean time, place B returned my call and asked if I was still interested in getting the information, in which I responded yes. (After all, I hadn't sent the contract to place A). I went to see place B and needless to say, this place was perfect *for me*.

Place B could accommodate up to five times the number of people for the same price that place A was offering. Immediately, I got excited. The place was so much nicer as well. I didn't know if this was the Lord providing for me *supernaturally* or if the enemy was playing tricks on me. How is this possible? But needless to say, I wanted everything that the Lord had for me and if He was going to provide this place for me for the same price, then of course, I was going to take the place that was more accommodating.

However, when I prayed about it, the Lord said, "Get what you need for where you are."

Make no mistake, it wasn't by happenstance that the fax for the contract to place A hadn't gone through – I was being tested to see if I was going to follow the Lord's instructions.

While the place was more cost effective, the accommodations were really way more than what I needed. So in obedience to the Lord's command, I went with the smaller, but accommodating place.

While Aaron was speaking to the whole Israelites community, they looked toward the desert, and there was the glory of the LORD appearing in the cloud.

The LORD said to Moses,

"I have heard the grumbling of the Israelites. Tell them, 'At twilight you eat meat, and in the morning you will be filled with bread. Then you will know that I am the LORD your God.'"

That evening quail came and covered the camp, and in the morning there was a layer of dew around the camp.

When the dew was gone, thin flakes like frost on the ground appeared on the desert floor.

When the Israelites saw it, they said to each other, "What is it?" For they did not know what it was. Moses said to them, "It is the bread the LORD has given you to eat.

Exodus 16:10 – 15 NIV

This bread from heaven, thin flakes like frost (white like coriander seed and tasted like wafers made with honey) was food, sent from God to feed the Israelites; His miraculous provision. However, when the Israelites saw it, they didn't know what it was and asked, "What is it?"

"It is the bread the LORD has given you to eat," Moses said.

I hate to even ask, in fact, I hate to even think about how many blessings I've missed because I didn't know what it was when it manifested; I didn't recognize it as being a blessing from the Lord; I didn't recognize it as being the blessing that I had been asking the Lord for, but had been complaining about (because I didn't have it). I thought, surely, the Lord hadn't heard my prayer because that's not what I asked for. And consequently, I missed the blessing because it wasn't what I thought it should've looked like.

We're so used to accepting whatever people give us or not wanting anything other than what we're used to getting that it's almost impossible for us to receive from the Lord. We're so used to the "natural" (what we can see, hear, taste, feel, or smell) that it's almost impossible for us to receive the "supernatural," you know, *the things of God.*

The people of Israel called the bread "Manna."

Exodus 16:31a NIV (emphasis added)

In the desert the whole community grumbled against Moses and Aaron. The Israelites said to them, "If only we had died by the LORD's hand in Egypt! There we sat around pots of meat and ate all the food we wanted, but you have brought us out into the desert to starve this entire assembly to death." That's right, the good ol' days, right? How many of us can look back now and see that they weren't so good after all?

How true it is that we become so accustomed to our situations, circumstances, and surroundings that we have no room for God's provisions for us. We've become so accustomed to this world's system that we have no room for God's supernatural provisions in our lives. We're so use to complaining and living in subpar situations that when the Lord provides for us we're unable to recognize it as a provision from the Lord. How is it that we've become so accustomed to the way we live that somehow, someway we think that this is the way to live and there is no other way?

We cry out for God to meet our needs, but it's according to how we dictate He should meet the need. How is it that we've become so dependent on the world's system that we can't receive from the God who created us and who came to give us life more abundantly?

How is it that all we can think about is the way it used to be, how things once were, and how things have always been? So much so, we have never even entertained the thought that there could be something better; that there could be a better way. I'm at the point now that there's **got to be** a better way.

How is it that we don't trust the God *who has made ways for us out of no ways?* How is it that we don't trust the God *who we say has saved us?* How is it that we don't trust the God *who we say has delivered us?* How is it that we don't trust the God *who we say has healed us?* How is it that we don't trust our God *who provides for us?*

How is it that we don't recognize the blessings of the Lord? We're so hung up on the natural that the supernatural is *unnatural.*

And this is the God we serve.

Why is it that the hardest thing for God to do for us is provide for us *miraculously?* How is it that we don't allow Him to provide *bread from heaven* for us?

While the Lord has provided bread from heaven to meet the needs of the Israelites, how is it that we don't allow the Lord to provide manna for us?

Manna means *what is it?*

What is it that you need? The Lord will provide.

Moses had to tell them what it was: "It is the bread the LORD has given you to eat."

And like the Israelites, we complain to God, we complain about God, and we ask for things that we think we need because that's what we're used to. We're so used to thinking what we've had is the best. We're so used to thinking that the way it was is the way it should always be.

Then when God answers our prayer, oh, I'm sorry, when God answers the complaint; we reject it because we have no idea what it is! Because it didn't come the way we thought it should come, because it doesn't look the way we think it should look.

We don't trust Him to meet our needs.

We're so used to getting what we want, how we want it, and when we want it; we're so wrapped up in ourselves and in the world's system that the truth is, we wouldn't be able to recognize a miracle if it slapped us in the face. Not to mention how we're supposed to receive a miracle.

We're crying out to God…for what?

What is it that you want God to do for you that you're open to receive? ***What is it*** that you want God to do for you that you're ready to receive? ***What is it*** that you want God to provide for you that you're willing to trust Him for it? ***What is it*** that you want God to do that you're willing to obey His commands?

What is it?

There are two things that you can count on in order to receive God's promise:

- ❖ He will provide for you supernaturally.
- ❖ You will be tested.

What is this?

The Lord is trying to get the Israelites to stop depending on the world's system and trust Him for supernatural provision! My God, why is that so hard to do? It's hard because *we don't know Him, we don't trust Him*, and *we won't renew our minds to the things of God.* We've been programmed or should I say "taught" to think it's okay to live in bondage. We've been "taught" to think that it's okay to live below the poverty line. We've been "taught" to think that the world's worse is God's best. We've been "taught" to think the government takes care of us better than God takes care of us!

How do we think we're going into the Promised Land that the Lord has given us when we don't even trust the Lord!

Somehow we've forgotten or somehow we've never been told that God promised to meet our needs just as He did for the Israelites in the desert. Somehow, we think that because He doesn't just *give us* what we want, when we want it – He's not God. Somehow, we think that God is going to just rain down manna; rain down whatever it is that we need and we'll just live in abundance. But we are sadly mistaken! And it's time for a wakeup call!

If you want it to rain down bread from heaven you've got to be tested.

Yes, the Lord will provide for you, but He's going to test your obedience. He wants to see if you'll obey his detailed instructions.

We can learn to trust him as our *Lord* by following Him; His instructions, His commands. We can learn to obey by taking small steps of obedience. And while I'd like to say it gets progressively easier and easier to trust Him, it doesn't – because we're tested on different levels. And I have to say that if you don't trust Him, you'll continue to get tested until you do.

"Be careful to obey all the commands I am giving you today. Then you will live and multiply, and you will enter and occupy the land the LORD swore to give your ancestors.

Remember how the LORD your God led you through the wilderness for these forty years, humbling you and testing you to prove your character, and to find out whether or not you would obey his commands.

Yes, he humbled you by letting you go hungry and then feeding you with manna, a food previously unknown to you and your ancestors. He did it to teach you that people do not live by bread alone; rather, we live by every word that comes from the mouth of the LORD."

Deuteronomy 8:1 – 3 NLT

Bread from Heaven was a type or foreshadowing of Jesus Christ, who is the "true bread from Heaven"

Jesus replied, "I tell you the truth, you want to be with me because I fed you, not because you understood the miraculous signs.

But don't be so concerned about perishable things like food. Spend your energy seeking the eternal life that the Son of Man can give you. For God the Father has given me the seal of his approval."

They replied, "We want to perform God's works, too. What shall we do?"

Jesus told them, "This is the only work God wants from you: Believe in the one he has sent."

They answered, "Show us a miraculous sign if you want us to believe in you. What can you do? After all, our ancestors ate manna while they journeyed through the wilderness! The Scriptures say, 'Moses gave them bread from heaven to eat.'"

Jesus said, "I tell you the truth, Moses didn't give you bread from heaven. My Father did. And now he offers you the true bread from heaven. The true bread of God is the one who comes down from heaven and gives life to the world."

"Sir," they said, "give us that bread every day."

Jesus replied, "I am the bread of life. Whoever comes to me will never be hungry again. Whoever believes in me will never be thirsty.

But you haven't believed in me even though you have seen me.

However, those the Father has given me will come to me, and I will never reject them.

For I have come down from heaven to do the will of God who sent me, not to do my own will.

And this is the will of God, that I should not lose even one of all those he has given me, but that I should raise them up at the last day.

For it is my Father's will that all who see his Son and believe in him should have eternal life. I will raise them up at the last day.

John 6:26 – 40 NLT

We have Jesus Christ, the bread from heaven that gives eternal life.

God is going to give you His word (*that's the manna*); His word. So when we're looking to God to provide for us supernaturally, often times we're looking for Him to "give" us "something" or "manifest" something; but I want to say to you that the **manna is the "word of God"** that is spoken; **that's** the miracle; the "word of God" that is manifested; **that's** the miracle.

Let's take a look:

Then the LORD said to Moses, "I will rain down bread from heaven for you."

The miracle, people of God is – the Word of God manifested. The manna, the supernatural provision, people of God is – the Word of God manifested. The Lord said it and it was so! It came to pass! His word manifested. He did just what He said He'd do.

But here's the stipulation: follow my instructions:

Each day the people can go out and pick up as much food as they need for that day. I will test them in this to see whether or not they will follow my instructions. On the sixth day they will gather food, and when they prepare it, there will be twice as much as usual."

- ❖ Each household should gather as much as it needs.
- ❖ Some gathered a lot, some only a little.
- ❖ But when they measured it out, everyone had just enough. Those who gathered a lot had nothing left over, and those who gathered only a little had enough. Each family had just what it needed.
- ❖ Do not keep any of it until morning.

But some of them didn't listen and kept some of it until morning. But by then it was full of maggots and had a terrible smell. *Moses was very angry with them. (They didn't follow his instructions.)*

I couldn't help but think about and come to the realization of what it actually means when you leave Egypt, which is reflective of "the world;" *you enter into the wilderness.*

Now, if Egypt represents the world, what does the wilderness represent?

The wilderness is the place of preparation. It is the place where God cares for us, provides for us, and teaches us to trust Him. It is the place where we learn to transfer our trust in the world's system onto God.

According to the Scripture, it's also a place of testing; to see if we'll do what the Lord is telling us to do. It is considered to be a place where the environment is hostile. It is a barren place; a place where we have nothing and have to depend on God to supply everything that we need; devoid, completely without. It is a place that allows God to build our character and mold us into who He has created us to be.

"If only the LORD had killed us back in Egypt," they moaned. "There we sat around pots filled

with meat and ate all the bread we wanted. But now you have brought us into this wilderness to starve us all to death."

Exodus 16:3 NLT

Being in the wilderness creates separation from the things of the world and the things of God. When God begins to do a work in us, the first thing that He does is remove us from that environment; the environment that we are *familiar* with; the environment that we *depend* on. He does this so that we *see, understand, and* come to the *realization* of how we are being affected by that environment. And to make us *aware* of what it is that we "value" and where our *loyalty* lies.

Ultimately, it's to show us, reveal to us our mindset, the way we think, the way we behave, what we believe. It is His attempt for us to get to know Him. Trust Him. Live for Him.

But because we have lived in that environment, the world's system, for so long, it's the only thing that we know; it's the *only* way of life that we're familiar with. And anything other than what we know, creates conflict within us and causes us to become unbalanced; unstable. In our attempt to hold on, like the children of Israel, we cry out for the familiar; we long for the familiar, which results in us prolonging our stay in the wilderness. Isn't it funny how we cry out to God to deliver us from a situation, and when He does, we cry out because we want to stay? I'm sure we, like the children of Israel, have cried out for God to deliver us, help us out of our situations, and when He does, we want to go back to where he delivered us from; where it's familiar. We fight to hold on then we fight to let go.

We want things to change, but we don't change things; *we* don't want to change. Who we are now attracts what's on the inside of us. For example: the financial debt that we're in is a result of us not managing our finances or not having the *education* of how to manage our finances.

Our financial debt is a result of us not being disciplined in the area of our needs versus our wants; so we get whatever we want, but have to borrow for what we need. And consequently, because there is a lack of financial education, we continue to make the same mistakes. Then we overcompensate because we're trying to satisfy our *lack* with "things" – so we remain in debt. *Things* can't satisfy the lack of knowledge; *things* can't satisfy the lack of value; *things* can't satisfy worth; *things* can't satisfy your spiritual drought; *things* can't satisfy your hunger for God.

The Israelites said, *"There we sat around pots filled with meat and ate all the bread we wanted."* While they remembered the pots filled with meat and eating all the bread they wanted, they forgot that they had to make brick without straw; they forgot that they had been whipped; they forgot about the hard labor; they forgot about the oppression; they forgot about being in bondage.

But we must understand that the desire for the "pots of meat" and "all the bread they could eat" isn't really about being in a place that was "so good," as much as it is about them longing for the familiar – no matter how bad it was. It was what they knew. It was all that they knew, and that's what they longed for. For them something familiar, no matter how devastating, was better than being in a place of unfamiliarity. And we're no different.

They had never been in a place where they had to solely depend on God; a God that they did not know; a God that they did not trust, in a place that they had never been. It was all new to them. And being in a new environment was now putting demands on them that they weren't familiar with.

An environment that demanded them to forget where they came from; forget what it was like; forget what they had been through; forget how it worked; forget how it was; forget how it used to be;

forget who they used to do it with; forget everything that they learned and lived in Egypt – the world's system – and trust God. And we're no different.

I can't help but be reminded of when the Lord was telling me to go to Orlando and my first thought was *I was going to die.* I'm laughing now, but I was terrified, just like the children of Israel. One thing for sure is *the fear* of leaving the familiar is overwhelming; leaving the only thing that you've known. I had never lived outside of Chicago, so to leave and go somewhere that I wasn't familiar with was very overwhelming and frightening. Just as overwhelming is the fear of the unknown; unknown territory.

You have no idea *what's* going to happen, *how* it's going to happen, or *if* it's going to happen. Being in a new environment is overwhelming, and I think it's safe to say that we all know what it's like to be in a new environment. While the environment may be different, the principle is the same; we are challenged in our very being, we are challenged to our core. Everything about us is challenged: mind, body, soul, and spirit.

The thing that we learn about the familiar is that it's difficult to leave. It's difficult to leave the people you're familiar with. It's difficult to leave the things that make you comfortable. It's difficult to leave the system that you've known all your life. It's difficult to leave the standard of living that you've struggle to maintain all of your life. Another thing that we learn about the familiar is that it's not *that difficult* that we *can't* leave. In order for us to do the things God is calling us to do, we have to leave; we *must* leave. We have to leave the people we know; we have to leave the familiar place; we have to leave the things that make us comfortable; we have to leave the system that has proven not to work for us; we have to leave the environment that causes us to remain stagnant; we have to leave the standard of living, the lifestyle that causes us to live below our means – below the abundant life that Jesus came to give us.

Even though our first response to the things of God, the unfamiliar, is usually *I want to go back to what's familiar,* God understands. However, while it's our first response, it can't be our *only* response. At some point we have to let go. At some point we have to move on. At some point we have to get to *know* the God we serve. At some point we have to trust Him. At some point our hesitation has to become definite. God wants the best for us. And if taking us out of our familiar environment in order to give us His best, then that's what He'll do. But we've got to want His best for us. We've got to want Him.

Then the LORD said to Moses, "Look, I'm going to rain down food from heaven for you. Each day the people can go out and pick up as much food as they need for that day. I will test them in this to see whether or not they will follow my instructions.

On the sixth day they will gather food, and when they prepare it, there will be twice as much as usual."

Exodus 16:4 - 5 NLT

Okay, let me make it personal: A test of your obedience – to His – detailed instructions. I wish I could say, "*Just* because you said, 'Yes,' He's going to give you what you need." But I can't. Although saying, "Yes" is the first step to getting what God has for you, it's not the only step. You have to do more than just say, "Yes." The Lord makes it absolutely clear that in order for us to receive the blessings, we will be tested. And not only will we be tested, but it goes without saying, we have to pass the test. Wait! I have to back up a little because I want you to see what the Lord revealed to me:

HE GIVES THE PROMISE

Then the LORD said to Moses, "Look, I'm going to rain down food from heaven for you. The Lord said He's going to give them what they asked for. In this case, the children of Israel were asking for food, so He said, He was going to rain down food from heaven. Therefore, I can't even begin to tell you how excited I am to say, "The Lord is going to give you what you've asked for." There is no doubt in my mind that He's going to do just what He said He would do. Whatever it is that you need, the Lord is going to give it to you, just like He did for the children of Israel. How do I know? We have His word: *He said so. And He did.*

Now, I couldn't help but notice that the Lord had done something that maybe most of us would've overlooked: *He revealed the end in the beginning. He revealed the promise in the beginning.* He gives us His word then He brings it to pass. What do I mean by "the end in the beginning"? He has revealed to us upfront that we're going to get the blessings. *Before the test,* He revealed we would get the blessing. It doesn't matter the test, we have His word; we have His promise that we will receive the blessings when it's all said and done. I can't help but be reminded of Joseph:

One night Joseph had a dream, and when he told his brothers about it, they hated him more than ever.

"Listen to this dream," he said.

"We were out in the field, tying up bundles of grain. Suddenly my bundle stood up, and your bundles all gathered around and bowed low before mine!"

His brothers responded, "So you think you will be our king, do you? Do you actually think you will reign over us?" And they hated him all the more because of his dreams and the way he talked about them.

Soon Joseph had another dream, and again he told his brothers about it. "Listen, I have had another dream," he said. "The sun, moon, and eleven stars bowed low before me!"

This time he told the dream to his father as well as to his brothers, but his father scolded him. "What kind of dream is that?" he asked. "Will your mother and I and your brothers actually come and bow to the ground before you?"

But while his brothers were jealous of Joseph, his father wondered what the dreams meant.

Genesis 37:5 – 11 NLT

We may all be familiar with Joseph's dreams, and, therefore, we know that the dreams did come to pass. Joseph did rule over his family: Pharaoh said to Joseph, "I hereby put you in charge of the entire land of Egypt." Only Pharaoh, sitting on the throne, was a higher rank than Joseph. But Joseph received the promise *first*. He received the word of God *first*. The Lord made His plan known *first*. He was going to bless Joseph. But, like the children of Israel, in order to receive the blessings, he had to be tested.

Until the time came to fulfill his dreams, the LORD tested Joseph's character.
Psalm 105:19 NLT

I can't help but be reminded of my own situation as well, which I talk about in great detail in my book, *Birthing Ministry*. How the Lord revealed that I was being promoted to a new level; a new level of power and authority, a new level in the prophetic; a new level of wisdom, a new level of praise and worship. And at the same time, He also revealed I was getting ready to be attacked – by Satan. There would be three different attacks that I had to endure – as He tested me to see if I would obey.

Until the time came to fulfill His promise, the LORD tested my character.

HE GIVES THE INSTRUCTIONS

When the Lord gave His promise, He also gave the instructions: **"Each day the people can go out and pick up as much food as they need for that day. On** *the sixth day they will gather food, and when they prepare it, there will be twice as much as usual."* Well, let me say it this way: when we get the promise, when the Lord gives us His word, we have to be obedient and do what He tells us to do. In doing so, not only is He testing us, not only is He proving our character, but we learn to trust Him; we get to know Him, and it increases our faith. The instructions are very detail oriented:

- ❖ Each day the people can go out and pick up as much food as they need for that day.
    - o Each day
    - o Go out
    - o Pick up as much food as they need
    - o For that day!
- ❖ On the sixth day they will gather food, and when they prepare it, there will be twice as much as usual.
    - o On the sixth day,
    - o Gather food
    - o Prepare it

Then Moses told them, "Do not keep any of it until morning."

Exodus 16:19 NLT

- ❖ Do not keep any of it until morning.
    - o Do not

- o Keep any
- o Until morning

But some of them didn't listen and kept some of it until morning. But by then it was full of maggots and had a terrible smell. Moses was very angry with them.

Exodus 16:20 NLT

He told them, "This is what the LORD commanded: Tomorrow will be a day of complete rest, a holy Sabbath day set apart for the LORD. So bake or boil as much as you want today, and set aside what is left for tomorrow."

Exodus 16:23 NLT

- ❖ Tomorrow will be a day of complete rest…So bake or boil as much as you want today, and set aside what is left for tomorrow.
  - o Tomorrow, Complete rest
  - o Bake or boil as much as you want
  - o Set it aside
  - o For tomorrow

Some of the people went out anyway on the seventh day, but they found no food.

The Lord asked Moses, "How long will these people refuse to obey my commands and instructions?

Exodus 16:27 – 28 NLT

HE GIVES THE TEST

I want to point out, unlike a "test" that we normally take, which is to determine if we pass or fail, the Lord is not "testing" us to see if we pass or fail. He's "testing" us to "prove" us; to show where our loyalty lies; to show us if we trust Him or not; to show us if we have faith in Him. *I will test them in this to see whether or not they will follow my instructions.* The "test" is to work out anything in *us* that doesn't line up with His word; His character.

❖ I will test them in this to see whether or not they will follow my instructions.
  o I will develop them
    ▪ I will teach them
  o In this
    ▪ by doing this
  o To see
    ▪ to reveal
  o Whether or not
    ▪ obedient or disobedient
  o They will follow my instructions
    ▪ trust or doubt

Testing brings out our character flaws, which allows God to develop us in those areas. So if we lack faith in Him, if we don't trust Him, when we're tested, the lack of trust will be revealed. Not for His sake, but for our sake. If we say we trust Him, but our actions say otherwise, the lack of faith will be revealed.

If we rely on the world's system that goes against dependence on God, the lack of confidence in God will be revealed. As these things are revealed to us and in us, this is how we mature in our relationship with God. If we trust Him, we'll obey Him. And taking small steps of obedience increases our faith in Him; it proves Him. As we take the small steps, He'll meet our need. Then we'll be encouraged to take the next step.

When the Lord provides for us, it allows us to see His glory, His character, His love for us. It reminds us that it is His good pleasure to bless us. And we show Him how thankful we are when we praise and worship Him.

When we're being "tested" ("proven" if you will), we get to see Him in ways that we've never seen Him before. We get to know Him in ways that we've never known Him before. We get to experience Him in ways that we've never experienced Him before.

Testing causes us to reflect on His goodness. It reminds us of how He has kept us and brought us through the difficult times in our lives. It reminds us of how faithful He has been in our lives. And we use those experiences, those difficult times, to encourage and remind ourselves that if He did it for us then, He'll do it for us now. Then we trust Him.

He *is* faithful.

Two
Financial Freedom

In an audible voice, the Lord spoke from Heaven and said, "Write a book."

Immediately, I knew the book would be about *financial freedom* when His words were spoken.

But just as suddenly as He made known what the book would be about, I, like Mary, (when the angel Gabriel announced she would conceive and give birth to a son) responded, "But how can this be?"

I knew absolutely nothing about financial freedom. *How am I going to tell somebody about financial freedom? What is financial freedom?* I wondered. Not only that but I was reminded of the type of books that I write, personal testimonies; personal experiences. And I hadn't been through anything; any oppression, hardship, battle, or warfare of any kind, so what was I going to write in the book?

Then there was an itty-bitty, tiny part of me that wondered *am I getting ready to go through something so that I can write this book?*

And sure enough, the *test* was before me.

The *pain of my past* surfaced.

And it proved to be too much for me; suddenly the tears were falling from my eyes as I struggled to keep *my* word of obedience – as the test began.

The LORD said, "I have indeed seen the misery of my people in Egypt. I have heard them crying out because of their slave drivers, and I am concerned about their suffering.

So I have come down to rescue them from the hand of the Egyptians and to bring them up out of that land into a good and spacious land, a land flowing with milk and honey – the home of the Canaanites, Hittites, Amorites, Perizzites, Hivites and Jebusites.

Exodus 3:7 - 8 NIV

The Lord has seen our misery, He has heard our cry and He's concerned about our suffering.

We are in financial ruin.

We are bankrupt financially.

And yet, we continue to struggle trying to make it day in and day out on our own. The Lord Himself has come down to rescue us from the hand of the Egyptians. Be it financial bondage, none the less, we are in bondage! The Lord Himself has come down to lead us out of Egypt; to lead us out of this world's system. It is the Lord's desire that we no longer trust in the world's system, but rather we trust in Him to provide for us; that He may lead us into a good and spacious land, a land flowing with milk and honey. Where we're no longer slaves, suffering at the hand of the enemy.

We're so focused on the fact that we have the first "African American" president that we've forgotten that when the housing market collapsed (and ultimately the collapse of the economy), hundreds of thousands, millions of people were out of jobs, and lost their homes. This same "African American" president bailed out the businesses that caused the collapse, but there was no relief for the people; there was no "straw" for the people. We had to make brick without straw.

That same day Pharaoh gave this order to the slave drivers and overseers in charge of the people:

"You are no longer to supply the people with straw for making bricks; let them go and gather their own straw.

But require them to make the same number of bricks as before; don't reduce the quota. They are lazy; that is why they are crying out, 'Let us go and sacrifice to our God.'

Make the work harder for the people so that they keep working and pay no attention to lies."

Exodus 5:6 – 9 NIV

We, the people, were left to try and make it on our own, the best way we knew how. And still we think that spending our days and nights depending on the world's system is somehow "making a way" for us. We work day and night and still live below the poverty line. We are depending on a system that wasn't created to support us, the people, but rather it was created for the people to support it.

In spite of the economy collapsing, we were still expected to produce! Make every mortgage payment, every car payment, every credit card payment, and every other financial obligation as well; in spite of *losing our jobs*, in spite of *losing our homes*. Imagine that. What's wrong with this picture?

Then the Israelite overseers went and appealed to Pharaoh: "Why have you treated your servants this way?

*Your servants are given no straw, yet we are told,
'Make bricks!' Your servants are being beaten, but
the fault is with your own people."*

Exodus 5:15 – 16 NIV

We found ourselves, as taxpayers, paying to get Wall Street, some of the largest financial institutions we have, out of debt; to keep the economy from completely collapsing. At least that's what we were told; to keep the economy from collapsing.

However, while it was apparent that the fault was with Wall Street; while it was apparent that the fault was with the financial institutions, there was no "bailout" for us, the people. And by the sweat of our brows we tried desperately to save ourselves.

We tried to make the mortgage payments, with no money; we tried to hold on to jobs that were closing their doors in our faces.

Beaten down, worn down with the misconception that there was no other way to save the economy *and* save us *at the same time.*

Pharaoh said, "Lazy, that's what you are – lazy! That is why you keep saying, 'Let us go and sacrifice to the LORD.'

Now get to work. You will not be given any straw, yet you must produce your full quota of bricks."

Exodus 5:17 – 18 NIV

Then, when we're looking for help, any kind of help, we have to hear that we're lazy and that we don't want to work! That we just want a hand out! That we just want something for nothing! When these very same financial institutions; presidents, vice presidents, and executives that used *our* tax dollars for the bailout, continued with the same practices that helped create the need for the bailout in the first place. They continued to give themselves hundreds of thousands, millions of dollars in bonuses while the world watched the economy teeter on the threat of complete collapse.

"Continue to make your mortgage payment," they said to us. "It doesn't matter that you don't have a job! You can get a job, *'they'* have jobs! *'They'* work hard and don't complain about the type of work they're doing." But there's no mention that *"they"* aren't citizens of the United States, and are getting paid in cash, in order to "beat" the system that's "designed" to keep "them" out.

God also said to Moses, "I am the LORD.

I appeared to Abraham, to Isaac and to Jacob as God Almighty, but by my name the LORD I did not make myself known to them.

I also established my covenant with them to give them the land of Canaan, where they resided as foreigners.

Moreover, I have heard the groaning of the Israelites, whom the Egyptians are enslaving, and I have remembered my covenant.

"Therefore, say to the Israelites: 'I am the LORD, and I will bring you out from under the yoke of the Egyptians. I will free you from being slaves to them, and I will redeem you with an outstretched arm and with mighty acts of judgment.

I will take you as my own people, and I will be your God. Then you will know that I am the LORD your God, who brought you out from under the yoke of the Egyptians.

And I will bring you to the land I swore with uplifted hand to give to Abraham, to Isaac and to Jacob. I will give it to you as a possession. I am the LORD.'"

Exodus 6:2 – 8 NIV

God is getting ready to do a new thing in our lives. He's getting ready to bless us with abundance. He revealed Himself to Abraham, Isaac, and Jacob as God Almighty, El-Shaddai. He never revealed Himself to them by His name "the LORD." They didn't know him as the LORD; they knew Him as God Almighty!

The Lord said, *"Then you will know that I am the LORD your God, who brought you out from under the yoke of the Egyptians."* In other words, then you will *know* that "I am the LORD" your God, who brought you out from under the yoke of the Egyptians.

If we remember, in Exodus, chapter three, verse fourteen, *And God said unto Moses, I AM THAT I AM: and he said, Thus shalt thou say unto the children of Israel, I AM hath sent me unto you.* Moses knew Him as "I AM," but now He was revealing Himself as "the LORD." Therefore, God was getting ready to use Moses to reveal Himself to the people so that they would come to know Him as "the LORD" *to establish a personal relationship with the people.*

After this presentation to Israel's leaders, Moses and Aaron went and spoke to Pharaoh. They told him, "This is what the LORD, the God of Israel,

says: Let my people go so they may hold a festival in my honor in the wilderness."

We're getting ready to get to know the LORD in a way that we've never known Him before. We're getting ready to get to know Him on an *even more personal level* than we've ever known Him before. We're getting ready to get to know His nature, His character – Him – period. We're getting ready to see His divine presence, provision.

I will test them to see if they will follow my instructions…

An Extraordinary Life

Well, like the rest of America, my husband and I found ourselves struggling to stay afloat financially. While he was the only one working at the time, we were doing well. Then suddenly he was out of a job. And as optimistic as we tried to be, things started to get bleak.

We, like the rest of America, had the mortgage payment, credit card debt, and other expenses. And we, like the rest of America, were struggling to pay the mortgage, credit card debt, and keep up with the other expenses as well. So much so, we, like the rest of America, were "robbing Peter to pay Paul."

We were drowning in debt when suddenly a life preserver was tossed out, and Randolph got a job at the Post Office. All be it, temporary, the night shift, and paying minimum wage, it was help none the less. And after several months of working at the post office, day in and day out, little by little Randolph started to dread the days of going into what he calls the "bowels" of employment.

You see, in the midst of our struggle, we never stopped praying and crying out to the Lord to help us. Then one day, the Lord showed up and posed a simple, but life-changing question to Randolph:

"Do you want an ordinary life or an extraordinary life?" He asked. If you want an ordinary life, I'll give you a permanent job at the Post Office. But if you want an extraordinary life, then I'll give *that* to you as well."

"I want an *extraordinary life,*" Randolph responded.

I couldn't help but be reminded of the man who had been by the pool of Bethesda; who had been sick for thirty-eight years:

Inside the city, near the Sheep Gate, was the pool of Bethesda, with five covered porches.

Crowds of sick people—blind, lame, or paralyzed—lay on the porches.

One of the men lying there had been sick for thirty-eight years.

When Jesus saw him and knew he had been ill for a long time, he asked him, "Would you like to get well?"

John 5:2 – 6 NLT

It seemed like a silly question to ask. Of course the man wants to get well. Of course Randolph would want the extraordinary life; who wants to continue to live like that?! However, it turns out, it wasn't that silly after all, for a number of reasons: there are a number of people who live the same way the man by the pool of Bethesda lives; there are a number of people who live the same way that Randolph and I were living – struggling, but they don't want to change. They don't *want* to get better. They don't *want* to live an extraordinary life.

Because we've become so accustomed to the way things are; because we've become so familiar with the way things are, we don't *want* to change.

And it wasn't long after that the Lord instructed Randolph, as He had instructed the man to *do something,* in order to be made whole; in order to have an extraordinary life, He wanted us to *move to Orlando, Florida.* To which I responded, "There is no way I'm going to go to another state, and I'm certainly not getting ready to sell my house."

And yet, we continued to struggle.

I will test them to see if they will follow my instructions….

A Lottery Ticket

One day the Lord revealed to me in a dream:

In a dream…

"Something" appeared to be "like" a lottery ticket in Randolph's wallet.

Now I have to say that I was confused and immediately wondered if Randolph had bought a lottery ticket in his desperate attempt to try to up-side our down-side situation. My only hope was that he had not because we didn't believe in playing the lottery; we felt that playing the lottery puts your trust in the "chance" that you would make it, instead of trusting in the Lord to provide for you.

So, when Randolph came into the room, I asked him, "Do you have a lottery ticket in your wallet?"

"Why would I have a lottery ticket in my wallet?" he questioned.

"I don't know. The Lord showed me that you have a lottery ticket in your wallet."

"No. I don't have a lottery ticket in my wallet," he assured me.

Then I inquired of the Lord, because I was certain that the Lord revealed there was a lottery ticket in his wallet. And as I inquired of the Lord, He revealed:

The interpretation of the dream...

The credit cards that were in Randolph's wallet had become like a lottery ticket. We had been putting our trust in the credit cards; putting our trust in the "chance" that we would be able to pull ourselves out of the financial hole that we were in, instead of trusting the Lord to provide for us. We were taking out cash advances on one card, then a cash advance off of another card. Not only were we robbing Peter to pay Paul, but we were robbing Paul to then pay Peter!

I shared this information with Randolph and immediately, we knew there was no way that we could continue to live like that. We decided right then and there that we would never again trust in credit cards. And knowing that there was nothing else we could do about our financial situation we fell down on our knees and prayed; giving our financial situation to the Lord.

For years we had taken pride in maintaining our 800+ credit scores and all that we had accomplished. But with that one decision, we knew all that we had "accomplished" was all about to come crashing down. And consequently, we resolved that whatever happened with the credit cards; whatever happened with our credit scores was now up to the Lord. We were done!

So we contacted all of the credit card companies and told them that we weren't able to make the payments on the credit cards and asked if there was any help that they could offer. They all said there was *nothing* they could do to help us because all of the accounts were current. The accounts had to be *delinquent* in order for them to help us. So that was that.

There was nothing we could do; there was nothing they could do, so we let the "cards" fall where they may. We had had enough! We wanted out! And this was our first step of trusting the Lord with our finances. This was our first step in becoming financially free; this was our first step of being released from financial bondage, from financial oppression. Whatever happens happens.

Again, the Lord reminded us that He wanted us to move to Orlando, Florida.

And yet, we continued to struggle.

Now, this is not to say that you cannot have credit or credit cards because you have to be able to "do business" in the world's system. We have to be able to make an "exchange" in the world's system. However, we are *in* the world, but we are not *of* the world. We don't live by the same principles that the world lives by; we live by Kingdom principles. Just like Jesus provided the coin in the fish's mouth, because they were required to pay taxes, Jesus will provide for us – so that we can operate in the world's system.

"However, we don't want to offend them, so go down to the lake and throw in a line. Open the mouth of the first fish you catch, and you will find a large silver coin. Take it and pay the tax for both of us."

Matthew 17:27 NLT

That's the miracle, Jesus provides *for us* to operate in the world's system; He'll give us whatever we need – *that's the Kingdom principle.*

I will test them to see if they will follow my instructions....

Sell Your Mercedes Benz

Although we were no longer "robbing Peter to pay Paul," we continued to struggle to just pay the mortgage, what credit cards we could and the other expenses that we had. However, the one thing we didn't have to worry about was the car note (by this time, the car had been paid off). We had gotten the car that we both desired for a very long time; a Mercedes Benz. I was reminded of how we just "went for it."

We went to the Mercedes Benz dealership and pulled over to "look." It was then that we decided that there was no reason that we couldn't have the desires of our heart. We were in position to do it, so we did it! We saw the car that we wanted and purchased it brand new. The car had about 7 miles when we purchased it (white with light gray interior). Then from out of nowhere, Randolph said, "The Lord said, 'Sell the car.'"

"What?" I questioned. "You've got to be kidding!"

"It's the only way that we'll be able to make it, unless you want to lose the house and live in the car."

It all had to be some kind of joke! How was this possible! I cried out to the Lord. I think we had the car for maybe two years. But none the less, it was the only way that we would be able to survive. And Randolph was still working at the post office, and dreading every minute of it.

Surely, we were ready for the extraordinary life because *this* wasn't it. So, Randolph did some research on the amount that we could expect from the sell.

There were several places that we went to that confirmed the amount that we could get. And with everything that we had in us, we sold the car. They cut us a check right then and there; we got in our Dodge Durango (which was also paid off), and went to the bank to deposit the check.

With the relief of selling the car, we lived off of the money (making sure, if nothing else, the mortgage was paid). Needless to say, it was heartbreaking and devastating. But there was no other way out. We had to take what we had, sell it, so that we could live; so that we could, at the very least, keep our heads above water.

When she told the man of God what had happened, he said to her, "Now sell the olive oil

and pay your debts, and you and your sons can live on what is left over."

2 Kings 4:7 NLT

And yet, we continued to struggle.

And still, the Lord was telling us to move to Orlando, Florida.

I will test them to see if they will follow my instructions….

Move to Orlando

During this time, Randolph continued to remind me that the Lord was prompting us to move to Orlando, Florida. Now, I have to admit that I was afraid. I had never lived anywhere outside of Chicago, and knowing that there were hurricane seasons in Florida terrified me.

I mean, I was so terrified that I was like the children of Israel in the wilderness; thinking the Lord was only taking us to Florida to die. As I ministered to the Lord, I cried out to Him because I was afraid; I didn't want to go to Florida. I poured out my heart to Him, tears streaming down my face as I bowed before Him, but He revealed that *it was already done in the spirit realm.*

Meaning, the next season in my life would be in Florida. And this move would lead me to my destiny; my purpose. Therefore, I had to play *catch up in the natural realm* with what was going on in the spirit realm. By going to Florida, I would be in the will of God.

In other words, moving to Florida *had to happen* – it was already done. So I had to come into agreement with what the Lord was doing in the spirit; I had to come into agreement with what the Lord was doing in my life. And when I had gotten *that* revelation, I was no longer afraid, but was ready to go.

This brings me to another point of us trusting God while in the wilderness. He's not only "testing" us to see if we'll follow His instructions; He's not only "proving" us so that our character can be developed, but He's also strategically positioning us for His will to be done in our lives.

He's positioning us so that we can receive the blessings that He has for us. And it allows us to come into agreement with the plans that He has for us, not the plans we have for ourselves. It allows us to Trust Him to lead and guide us because He knows what's best for us.

Our Father which art in heaven, Hallowed be thy name. Thy kingdom come. Thy will be done, as in heaven, so in earth.

Luke 11:2b KJV

I had finally come around and realized it was time to go. It was time to move to Orlando, Florida as the Lord had revealed.

The LORD had said to Abram, "Leave your native country, your relatives, and your father's family, and go to the land that I will show you.

So one Saturday we woke up, and out of nowhere we decided we were going to go to Florida. So we rented a car, took our son with us and drove 18 hours to Florida (to the apartment complex that Randolph had researched). When we arrived at the apartment complex, we decided it wasn't the complex we wanted to live in. So we went to the nearest hotel and rented a room so that we could rest a little bit.

We asked the gentleman at the front desk about the surrounding area and where we could find an apartment. Our son chose to stay in the room to sleep while we went to look at the apartment the young man suggested. The apartment was absolutely beautiful and we were sooo excited. But the high school in that district was a "D" rated school, so we ended up going to another complex where the high school was an "A" rated school.

We ended up going through the application process to rent the two-bedroom apartment. Of course they had to do a credit check to see if we qualified and if we'd have to put down a deposit. Initially, the gentleman said, "You're going to need a deposit."

But our immediate response was, "Oh, no, that couldn't be right. There should be no reason we would need a deposit, will you double check that because something's wrong, somewhere."

"Okay, let me double check it," he said. "I was looking at it and I'm not sure why it's saying that you need a deposit."

Eventually, we ended up signing the lease for the apartment (without a deposit), went back to the hotel, got our son, got back in the car, hit the road, and drove 18 hours back to Chicago, and started packing. Surely, it was the grace of God that took us and brought us back. (It's funny now when I think about it, but I remember talking to my sister-in-law on the phone the next day and telling her how we had just been to Florida and back. And she was like, "When?" in disbelief.

"Yesterday," I said. "We left Saturday morning and came back Sunday."

"Girl," she said. "I remember when you guys bought your house. And we were asking where are you guys moving to? And y'all were like, 'we don't know where, but when we see the house, we'll know that's it.'" She'd always talk about the "crazy faith" Randolph and I have. And how any time the Lord told us to do something, we just did it!

Then we started telling our family and friends that we were moving; going to Orlando. And the responses were all the same: Who do you know in Florida? Do you have a job? Where are you going to live? What about your house? And our response was always the same: We have no family, no friends, no jobs, no money, and had no idea what was to become of the house. (While we were in the process of trying to rent the house out, things had started to get shaky with the young lady coming up with the rent and deposit, so we weren't sure if she was going to rent it or not.)

Then people started blessing us financially. One day my aunt called, "Make sure you don't leave before I get there, I'm on my way over there." And when she arrived, she gave me a pink, razor phone (so that we'd at least have a phone). "You know I can't let you guys get on the road and you not have a phone for us to reach you," she said. And I just cried and cried because I *realized* we had absolutely nothing! We couldn't even afford to buy a phone. But God had provided. (And she ended up paying the telephone bill for the duration of the two-year contract.)

We had no idea what was getting ready to happen. But the one thing we did know – we were being obedient to the voice of the Lord. So we rented a truck, sold and/or gave away furniture that wouldn't fit in the two-bedroom apartment, packed up everything else, and headed out. Randolph drove the rental truck and I drove the Durango with our son.

We left Chicago and went to Orlando, Florida.

I will test them to see if they will follow my instructions....

Rest

Once we arrived in Orlando, we lived like we were on vacation. The apartment complex had a swimming pool, hot tub, racquet ball, basketball, and a workout center available to the residents. And every day was the same: wake up, eat, hang out at the pool, take a nap, wake up, eat, hang out at the pool, play racquet ball, workout, then eat, and go to sleep, for about three months.

We weren't concerned about getting jobs, we weren't concerned about how we were going to eat, or pay the rent; somehow, someway, God provided for us. We never worried about the credit card payments, and by the grace of God, the young lady had rented the house, so the mortgage was being paid.

All we had was Randolph's unemployment checks from the post office.

Later we came to realize that it was a period of rest for us.

The king and all who were with him grew weary along the way, so they rested when they reached the Jordan River.

2 Samuel 16:14 NLT

I can't even begin to tell you how devastating the impact was on me making the transition. I can't even begin to tell you how difficult it was for me to be in this place; a foreign land. The many nights I cried, as I longed to go back home to be with my family, were heart-wrenching. And if the truth be told, although I was in this place, although the Lord led us here, it was not home. At some point, I was sure the Lord would lead us back home. However, *it was clear that we had come to Florida on an assignment, and once the assignment was over, we'd go back home* I thought. When? I had no idea.

By this time, the credit card payments had become delinquent, so we called the credit card companies to see if there was anything they could do to help us? *Now* there was nothing they could do to help us because *we didn't have jobs;* we didn't have *any* income to make a payment of any kind. But we kept calling.

I remember one phone call in particular: I was asking the young lady if they could help me by at least lowering the payment. She advised me that in order to determine how much I would qualify for my monthly payment, we had to do a budget sheet, which I had to list all of my debt. By the end of the conversation the lady said, "Ma'am, you can't even afford to make *any* payment." It was true. And eventually, we just let it go.

Because I had gotten a new telephone number when my aunt gave me the telephone, there weren't any harassing telephone calls from the credit card companies. However, I ended up getting sued by *one* company. While they didn't have my telephone number, they had found my address. They came to my apartment to serve me the papers. So, off to court I went to respond. And let me tell you, they didn't care that I wasn't working, they wanted their money.

We worked out payment arrangements and eventually I paid the account off. The reality was, I knew I owed a debt and I was going to pay. (Once we got jobs, we paid all the balances that were outstanding. It didn't matter what it did to our credit, we had an outstanding debt, so we paid them.) After that, we decided we would never use credit cards again. If we couldn't pay cash for whatever we wanted, then we didn't need it.

I will test them to see if they will follow my instructions….

Go To Work

The time came for us to start looking for jobs, so we started sending our resumes out. And with each opportunity we were afforded, the pay was minimum wage. I started to get frustrated because I had management experience (but I wasn't getting any management opportunities). Then, finally, I got a phone call about a management position. The gentleman said he was very impressed with my resume and was really interested in offering me the position; however, based on where I lived, it would be a two hour drive for me, and therefore, he wasn't able to offer me the position.

Desperate, I was like, I'll drive two hours just give me the job. But he didn't, which added to my frustration because he knew my address before he called me! I couldn't help but wonder *what was that all about?*

I continued to get offers for minimum wage jobs, nothing close to what I was looking for. Then one day Randolph and I were talking, and in my frustration I said, "How are they going to offer me minimum wage when they see I have management experience!"

"You may have management experience, but you don't have a degree," he responded. "That's why they're offering you minimum wage."

"Well, I'm going to get my degree," I said. And immediately went out and registered for school to complete my bachelor's degree. While all I could see was frustration from getting minimum wage offers, the Lord was using that opportunity to get me to the next level; the Lord was using that opportunity to get me to take the next step in my life; earning my degree.

Get Your Degree

Well, the classes started and we were taking classes during the day and in the evening every week, at the campus. We were barely making it because the truck had started acting up. We felt lucky we had found a mobile mechanic. So any time we had problems with the truck we didn't have to worry about trying to get the car to the shop, but rather the mobile mechanic would come to us.

The problems started out as small problems, but quickly became more than we could afford, and eventually we would just ride it out. One by one, the motors to each window gave out, so we couldn't let the windows down. If you did, then you couldn't get it back up. Then the one window wouldn't stay up (we had to put a screw driver in it to stop it from falling down. We were so glad that the windows were tinted so you couldn't see the screw driver.

Then the air conditioner went out. And let me tell you, the ninety degree weather every day had no mercy on us. By the time we made it to the campus for class, we were about to pass out because it was so hot; but we pressed on. Although we only had classes at the campus three days out of the week (we were taking three/four classes at a time). We were at the campus everyday because we couldn't afford the internet. So, that meant, the majority of our days were spent at the school all day, from 8:00 a.m. to 10 p.m., either in the library or in the computer lab, (in between classes) trying to get our assignments done.

In the meantime, we continued to look for jobs. Then Randolph found out about a job fair at one of the convention centers in the area. So we went to the job fair and, as job fairs go, we gave our resumes to the companies we were interested in, and waited to see if we'd receive a call. And I did. The one company called. And while I had accepted the fact that I wasn't going to get the pay I wanted, at least it wasn't minimum wage. It was a position for a Customer Service Representative, in a call center, and I think it was twelve dollars and something an hour. Well, needless to say, I took it.

Then I had school three days a week on top of working full-time. Now, I must say, the job did provide some relief because I was able to use the internet at work to do my assignments, while Randolph continued to go to the school, which wasn't far from the job. Anyway, a couple of months later, Randolph got a job at the same place where I was working. So, things started to turn around for us and we were starting to get back on our feet.

And as I mentioned, the Lord made it clear that the first order of business was to pay the debts we owed for the credit cards. Even though it had been several months since the credit cards had been delinquent, and were now with collection agencies, we had to pay the debts. So we started paying off the credit card balances until one by one, the accounts had all been paid. It didn't matter that our credit had been affected. It didn't matter that the balances would eventually just get written off. The only thing that mattered was we owed a debt, and we were going to satisfy the debt.

Then we started to make plans for that "rainy" day.

Then Joseph said to the people, "Look, today I have bought you and your land for Pharaoh. I will provide you with seed so you can plant the fields.

Then when you harvest it, one-fifth of your crop will belong to Pharaoh. You may keep the remaining four-fifths as seed for your fields and as food for you, your households, and your little ones."

Genesis 47:23 – 24 NLT

When the Lord so graciously brought us to Orlando, and gave us our jobs, we felt prompted to start saving for that "rainy" day. And consequently, we created what we called the "Joseph Funds." One-fifth of our income, like Joseph had provided, was seed that the Lord had given us.

And every time we got paid it was harvest time, it went into a savings account that would allow us to live on. As it was revealed to Pharaoh in a dream through Joseph's interpretation of the dream, he was to collect one-fifth of all the crops during the seven good years. So, as we worked during the seven good years, we saved for the Joseph Funds.

And by the grace of God, all was going well at school; maintained a 4.0 G.P.A. Promotions on the job came quickly. My first promotion came after about six months on the job, so our finances increased quickly. Thank God because the tenant got crazy, wasn't paying the rent, so we had to pay the mortgage. I mean, it was one thing after the other with this girl.

When it was all said and done, we ended up going to Chicago to inspect the property. When we entered the property, to our surprise, the girl had taken the refrigerator, the TV that we let her son use, and she was trying to take the bunk bed that we let her son use. The only thing that stopped her from taking the bunk bed was you needed a special tool to unscrew the screws. But it was clear she was trying to get it down. Anyway, we ended up evicting her from the property; therefore, paying the mortgage fell on us until we were able to find someone else to rent it.

After about two years, we ended up getting a new car.

After three years, all was going well on the job. I had been promoted several times and was now working in Quality Assurance. And we had finally completed our bachelor's degrees in Business Administration with a concentration in Small Business Management and Entrepreneurship. So now that I had my degree, I was ready to get a "real" job; ready to get back out in the "real" work force.

One day, there was a job fair at the school. So I attended the job fair, and again, gave my resume to the companies that I was interested in. The school had a representative at the job fair, so I gave my resume to the representative as well. And again, I waited to see who would call – now that I had my degree. Well, I got a call from the school. The position was for an Admissions Advisor, paying about $10,000.00 more than what I was making, with a $3,500.00 starting bonus after ninety days, and 100% tuition paid for any degree I complete (and 90% tuition paid for Randolph). I took the job.

And just as quickly, Randolph continued to get promotions as well, and was working in the corporate office. As soon as we completed our bachelor's degrees, we enrolled in classes to start working on our masters degrees. Again, we were taking three/four classes at a time. After a year, we finished our degrees, M.B.A. in International Business (*free* for me, *and 90% tuition paid for Randolph*). Then we set our sights on completing our doctorate degrees.

We continued to focus on getting someone in and out to rent the house, and in the interim, the responsibility of the mortgage payments fell on us. Finally, after about a year, we finally got someone in the house who was trustworthy and committed to taking care of the property.

I will test them to see if they will follow my instructions….

Quit Your Job

So, all was going well. We had finally gotten back to a place of peace; where we were comfortable. The jobs were going well. Again, promotions came quickly. We were making about $100,000.00, finished our M.B.A.s, and all was well with the house. The Lord had kept His promise; He provided our every need.

One day while on the way to work, Randolph and I were talking. At that time, I was in the process of writing another book. And I mentioned to him that I was a little apprehensive about finishing the book. And as always, he encouraged me, "By the time you finish the book, you won't be at that job." And immediately, his words hit my spirit and I knew the words were prophetic. And consequently, I held them in my heart and waited for the word to come to pass.

It didn't take long for the Lord to confirm His word as I had pondered it in my heart. While walking down the hallway at work one day, I was arrested in my spirit, apprehended, as the word of the Lord came to me. The Lord said, "By the time you finish the book, you won't be at that job." I made an audible gasp, and immediately looked around to see if anyone heard me. I was in awe of the voice of the Lord, as the word was confirmed by the vision that was before me. And for a few seconds I was unable to move. It wasn't until the vision was taken away that I felt released to move forward.

As I pondered what the Lord had just said, my immediate thought was that I would be getting a new job. Instantly, I got excited. First and foremost, I wasn't going to be working at that place much longer, and secondly, I would have a new job; a better position and higher pay. Mere words could not express how excited I was, and yet I kept the word of the Lord to myself. However, I felt at liberty to share that my time at that place of employment was coming to an end, although I didn't know when.

I started sending my resumes out again to companies I was interested in, and waited to see who would call. But this time, the call never came. Then I started filling out applications for positions that were available within the company. I remember the first time I applied for a position, it was located in Tampa. I knew I wasn't going to be at that job much longer, so I started looking for opportunities that I believed were for me. I completed the application process, which had to go through Human Resources for approval. As I waited to see if I would be selected for an interview, I received an email.

However, the email indicated I had missed the deadline for submitting my application. When I went to Human Resources to see what happened with my application, I was advised that the application had been submitted and they had no idea what happened.

Anyway, I didn't challenge it; I just figured the position wasn't for me (besides, I didn't really want to move). Then another opportunity came up; I submitted my application. This time, I wanted to make sure my application was received in a timely manner – before the deadline. When I went to Human Resources, I was advised that the application hadn't been submitted as of yet, in fact, they didn't even know where the application was (as they searched their office for where they may have put it). Then asked if I could submit it again and they'll be sure to process it right away.

Needless to say, while I wasn't sure if the application was ever sent, I wasn't selected for the interview process. Then, I was approached by the Senior Director. She advised me that there was a position available that would include not only working with undergraduate students, but graduate students as well; a blended learning opportunity, and mentioned she thought it would be a good position for me, if I was interested.

Immediately, I was excited about the opportunity, and quickly got my documentation together to submit my application to Human Resources for approval. Now, because the Senior Director told me about the position, I figured, I pretty much had the position in the bag, so I wanted to make sure I stayed on top of the process. I couldn't let it slip through my fingers. I had to stay on top of Human Resources. So a couple of days after I submitted the application, I followed up with Human Resources. And to my surprise, I was asked, "Why did you submit your application for that position because the position isn't available."

"Not available?" I questioned.

"No, it's not."

"What do you mean? When was the deadline?"

"Well, from what I understand the position was never available. There is a freeze on hiring."

"What?!" Then I went on to share that the Senior Director told me the position was available and suggested I apply for it.

"The Senior Director?" she asked confused. "I spoke to the Director of the position and was advised that there aren't *any* positions available because of the freeze."

"You've got to be kidding me," I responded. I was just as confused; I had no idea what was happening.

And still, nothing.

And even so, I knew at some point, I would be leaving that job. When it would happen or how, I didn't know, but I knew it would. Then suddenly, my only desire and focus was leaving the job. And I was excited that I was going on to something bigger and better. However, as I sat and waited for the word of the Lord to come to pass, things on the job started to go downhill, fast.

WHERE IS THE MANNA?

Even though my time on the job was coming to an end, I didn't know exactly when. Therefore, I wanted to be able to take advantage of every opportunity that was available to me while I was there. I mean, there was absolutely nothing else I could do in the position I was in – that I hadn't already done. So I figured the best thing for me to do was to look for a promotional opportunity. And when the opportunity presented itself, a position for an Assistant Director, I decided that I would apply for it.

While there were a number of individuals who were just as qualified for this position, and had applied for it, I felt confident that I would be successful in getting the position. So when I was advised that I was selected as a potential candidate to interview for the position, I was excited.

Immediately, I focused on getting my ducks in a row. I reached out to the Assistant Directors and asked if I could meet with them to ask some questions that would help prepare me for the interview process. I reached out to my previous manager, who was now the Director of Operations, and asked for a letter of recommendation. I also asked a couple of professors from my M.B.A. program for letters of recommendation as well. And at that time, there was only one Executive Advisor in the department, who expressed his interest in seeing *me* get the position; therefore, I asked him for a letter of recommendation as well. I was ready. This job was mine.

The interview process consisted of all potential candidates interviewing with three different Directors within the department. Consequently, I interviewed for the position and was excited throughout the process as I was encouraged by each of the directors. Now, as with any position that was available within a company, it wasn't until after all of the potential candidates had been interviewed that we'd know which candidates were chosen for the next phase in the process.

The day had finally come. It was announced that we'd be meeting with the directors and the Human Resources Specialist to find out if we had been chosen. And one by one, we went in to find out if we had been selected to move forward in the next phase. It was understood that there would only be three people selected to move forward in the next phase of the process.

Now I have to say, there was no doubt in my mind that I was going to be one of the three. I was one of the top producers in the company, and the majority of the people that worked there also thought, surely, I was going to be one of the ones selected.

And one by one, each of us were called into the office where the interview process was being conducted, and the first few people that came out had not been selected. So needless to say, it started to get interesting. Then, another person went in. This time, the person had been selected. The rest of us kept track of who hadn't gone in as of yet, while also taking note of who *really* had the best shot at being selected. Anyway, at that point, we knew there were two more slots available to be filled. And after a few more people, there was only one slot available, but still a couple more people.

Then it was time for my scheduled appointment. I went in just as confident as I had throughout the interview process. And before I could even sit down, one of the directors started by saying how I had made the entire process a very difficult process; because they had no idea that I had so much to offer. During my time of employment, I had worked with one of the directors before, and the other directors were fairly new, and consequently, wasn't as familiar with my full potential. Anyway, the director continued. And I have to say, I was excited to hear the words of encouragement.

Basically, I was "the best thing since sliced bread." Then the other directors also had an opportunity to say how my skills and knowledge had not only been a huge contribution to the company, but would be coveted by any manager looking for someone to work with. And suddenly, almost as if interrupting the director as she spoke, the initial director said, "However, you were not selected to move forward to the next phase of the interview process."

Shocked and completely caught off guard, I said, "Thank you for your time and consideration," as I walked out of the room. I couldn't get back in the office fast enough before everyone had bombarded me, asking if I had been selected. "No. I wasn't selected," I said in disbelief.

"What?!" they all responded.

We all knew that my selection was in the bag. Therefore, we were all in total shock, to say the least. I went on to share with them how I really felt like I had been blind-sided. I mean, all of the words of encouragement, and then, from out of nowhere, '...you were not selected to move forward in this process.' I did not see that coming, and was completely baffled.

Anyway, there wasn't anything I could do about the decision, so I let it go. Then, I decided that I'd find out from each of the directors what skills they thought I needed to work on, so when the opportunity became available again, I'd be ready. After a few days, I reached out to the directors to find out why I hadn't been selected, and if they could give me some feedback. And when no one was able to tell me why I wasn't selected to move forward in the process, I was just as shocked as I was when I initially heard that I hadn't been selected. And yet, I continued to reach out to them. If nothing else, someone was going to tell me why I hadn't been selected. And to my dismay, there weren't any answers.

Until finally, I was advised by my manager, that one of the potential candidates had been through the process before and was advised that if she worked on some specific skills, she'd be chosen to move forward when the opportunity presented itself again. And consequently, she had "worked on her skills" and was then chosen to move forward. Therefore, because she had been promised a spot in the selection process, she was chosen (not me). And apparently, the other two individuals beat me out.

Nonetheless, after the interview process had been completed, "management" decided that they were not going to fill the position after all. So, ultimately, no one got the job. However, that just meant, the next time the position became available, we pretty much knew who was the biggest competition. For me, the two initial candidates that were chosen were my biggest competitors. But that meant nothing to me. I was going to step my game up and be ready when the position became available again.

And then it happened. After a year, not only had the position become available again, but there were three positions that management was looking to fill. Okay, so I got this one in the bag. And the time started to draw near for anyone who was interested to apply or reapply (if they had been a part of the initial process). Well, let me say this, *a lot can happen in a year.*

I had become that much more dissatisfied with being on the job, and that much more excited about the Lord blessing me to work in full-time ministry. And the Lord began to minister to me concerning the Assistant Director position; He reminded me that my time on the job was limited. And while I didn't *really* want the job, but *really* wanted God to release me, still, I had no idea how much time was meant by "limited." *I was torn.*

And yet, I didn't know how much more of that job I could take; especially if I had to stay in that same position. And the tears that fell from my eyes were a testament to my need for the Lord to step in and do something. "If you want me to do full-time ministry, release me!" I cried out.

"Move on," he responded.

And immediately, I was reminded of Moses leading the children of Israel:

Then the Lord said to Moses, "Why are you crying out to me? Tell the Israelites to move on."

Exodus 14:15 NIV

I understood the Lord was telling me to stay focused on what He had called me to do. 'Move on.' Clearly, He wasn't interested in entertaining me and my desires that had nothing to do with what He had called me to do; that had absolutely nothing to do with where He was taking me; that had absolutely nothing to do with my destiny.

Therefore, it was my responsibility to stay focused as I waited for Him to release me. It was also clear that while I had been crying out to the Lord for Him to release me, I had to also make sure I was *doing* what He told me to do, in order to be released. I knew what the Lord had called me to do and it didn't include getting promoted on my job. So in essence, I needed to take my eyes off the job, and focus on ministry. In other words, He was saying, "Stop crying out to me and do what I've told you to do!" (And that was to prepare for my release.)

I had been encouraged, strengthened, and refocused. My only concern and focus at that point had to be ministry. And while my heart understood and was more than happy to oblige, it was a little more difficult for my mind to come into agreement. And consequently, I knew my time on the job was limited, but I wanted the promotion, I wanted the increase. And it became that much more difficult for me to settle in my mind that I had decided to follow Jesus. Then I had a dream:

In the dream...

I saw the plant on my desk at work. It started to bud and flowers started to grow on it.

Immediately, when I woke up, I was reminded of Aaron's staff:

Then the LORD said to Moses,

"Tell the people of Israel to bring you twelve wooden staffs, one from each leader of Israel's

ancestral tribes, and inscribe each leader's name on his staff.

Inscribe Aaron's name on the staff of the tribe of Levi, for there must be one staff for the leader of each ancestral tribe.

Place these staffs in the Tabernacle in front of the Ark containing the tablets of the Covenant, where I meet with you.

Buds will sprout on the staff belonging to the man I choose. Then I will finally put an end to the people's murmuring and complaining against you."

So Moses gave the instructions to the people of Israel, and each of the twelve tribal leaders, including Aaron, brought Moses a staff.

Moses placed the staffs in the Lord's presence in the Tabernacle of the Covenant.

When he went into the Tabernacle of the Covenant the next day, he found that Aaron's staff, representing the tribe of Levi, had sprouted, budded, blossomed, and produced ripe almonds!

Numbers 17:1 – 8 NLT

And I understood that just as Aaron had been chosen, I was chosen. Clearly because the plant on my desk was a Pothos; Epipremnum, a leaf plant, it doesn't produce flowers. The Lord had chosen me for ministry. You see, this was it. This was going to be the start of what I had been hoping for, dreaming of, and believing for, full-time ministry. And as long as I stayed focused, I would have what He had promised.

And somehow it all started to make sense. That's why no one could tell me why I wasn't selected for the interview process – because God said, "No." The Lord had other plans on His mind concerning me. And even so, it wasn't that easy to just walk away; especially when I thought about the additional money that the position would afford me.

At the time the position was being offered, it would've been a fifteen thousand dollar increase, and that wasn't easy to walk away from. And just as equally difficult to walk away from, was my desire to do ministry. It was a difficult decision. And to make matters worse, it was that much more difficult to continue doing what I was doing in my current position. I mean, it took everything that I had within me just to get up and go to the job.

However, as difficult as it was for me to walk away from the fifteen thousand dollar increase, the Lord comforted me. As I sat thinking about it, my thoughts were interrupted…

"I will repay," He said. And the tears fell from my eyes as I wondered, *how much longer do I have to stay on this job!* His words: powerful and established. It was settled. I was not going to get the promotion or the increase that I had desired. His will had to be done.

There was no doubt in my mind that if I walked away from the promotion and the increase, He would repay. I had His word. He would make a way for me to get it back, one way or another; however He chose to bless me. I was willing to walk away. But because of the constant reminder, because of the temptation I went back and forth with my decision for a little while. And just as frequently, I'd hear the voice of the Lord, "I will repay." But I had come to the end of my rope in my position. And if something didn't give, I didn't know how it was all going to play out.

Finally, it was settled in my heart, I believed the Lord.

Now, little did I know – my faith would be tried.

The position was finally posted, and everyone that was interested had started to submit their applications for consideration. I was strengthened by the fact that I wasn't going to apply for the position. That, in itself, would prove to be my first step towards victory; taking God at His word. Then, as usual, everyone started asking around to find out who had submitted their application for consideration. And every time someone asked me if I had submitted my application, I was happy to respond, "No. I'm not interested."

Then, I felt the need to 'explain' that my time on the job was limited. I was looking forward to doing full-time ministry. When no further response was needed after hearing that I was going into full-time ministry, I thought, *Okay. That wasn't all bad.* So it wasn't a long drawn out conversation about why I wasn't interested in the position. My faith in what the Lord told me to do was strengthened.

However, *my faith* didn't stop me from sitting at my desk every single day trying desperately to convince myself that *I had made the right decision.* And just when I thought I had escaped the grasp of the temptation that refused to let me go, my manager called me into the office.

"I was advised that you haven't applied for the Assistant Director position as of yet," he said.

Not only had I not applied, but I wondered *why* "the person" was concerned that I hadn't applied. I was convinced that "the person" *wanted* me to apply, which my manager went on to confirm.

"I just want to share with you," he said, "that the two people that initially had the upper hand on you in the first round, well, that's not the case anymore. You should apply. You'll be surprised at the outcome."

I knew the job was mine. Certainly, he confirmed that if I wanted it, I could have it. But it took everything that I had within me just to utter, "No thanks, I'm not interested."

"You're not going to apply?" he asked surprised. Because he knew I was gunning for that position. "I'm telling you," he continued, "things are not the same as they were a year ago. And without saying too much, trust me; you'll be surprised at the outcome."

"No," I said with as much certainty as I could muster; the temptation was so enticing.

"Why not?"

"Because I'm no longer interested; my interest is elsewhere." And while I thought it was sufficient to just say that *I wasn't interested,* I felt compelled to say *why* I wasn't interested (almost as if it was going to *solidify* the decision that I made).

"Are you looking for another job?"

"No. I'm interested in full-time ministry."

"Oh, okay. Well, I'm not going to try to convince you. I know how it is if you've got your mind set on something else. I respect that."

"Thanks."

And just as I put my hand on the door knob to leave, immediately, all the strength that I had, left. Instantly, I became weak and wasn't sure if I was going to be able to make it back to my office; especially since my mind had drawn a complete blank. But the threat of tears rolling down my face caused me to muster whatever strength I could in order to keep my manager from seeing me cry.

Somehow I had made it. And immediately, I turned looking through my files, which gave the tears an opportunity to fall while my back was turned. "Please Lord," I cried. "Strengthen me." I had done what I committed to doing and needed to be strengthened to make it through the rest of the day.

Walking away from the promotion and the increase was far more difficult than I had imagined. But I did it. In spite of the promotion, in spite of the fifteen thousand dollar increase, in spite of not knowing how much longer I would be on the job, which had now turned to dread, there was something deep down inside of me that believed the Lord and wanted what He promised me.

The book that I had been working on was finally finished. I was excited for more reasons than one. The Lord said, 'by the time I finished the book, I would no longer be working at that job!' I was closer to leaving the job than I had ever been! The book hadn't been edited at that time, but none the less, it was finished in form, concept. Anyway, as the time passed, the book was going through the editing process.

Now, a friend of mine shared with me what she had heard during bible study, but first, I have to say that in all fairness, this particular preacher isn't someone that I normally listened to. Let's just say that he's not my "go to" *man of God* when I need a word or a breakthrough. Anyway, during her bible study, the man of God said that the Lord was going to visit us in a dream that night, and give us the instructions on how to move forward. And in the dream, the Lord was going to give us everything that we needed to know in order to get to the next dimension.

I know I've said it time and time again, but I have to say it again – I was desperate! Long story short, I received the word of the Lord and couldn't wait to prove the word. I needed the Lord to say something! I was really at the end of my rope – I was about to let go! *That* night before going to bed, I told the Lord that I was *expecting* Him to show up and give me all the information that I needed to move forward in what He had called me to do – as the man of God said.

Well, the next day when I woke up for my 3 a.m. devotion, I realized that I hadn't had a dream as the man of God said I would. So, I said to the Lord, "Lord, I'm expecting you to show up and give me the answers that I need to move forward in what you've called me to do – as the man of God promised."

And I went back to bed. When I went back to sleep, the Lord showed up and revealed Himself in a dream:

In a dream…

There was a man and a girl. The man asked the girl if she'd partner with him in his business. The girl agreed that she'd partner with him.

When I woke up, immediately, I understood the Lord was asking me to partner with Him. And He confirmed His word:

God will do this, for he is faithful to do what he says, and he has invited you into partnership with his Son, Jesus Christ our Lord.

1 Corinthians 1:9 NLT

In other words, in order to do what God had called me to do, fulfill my passion, my purpose, I had to go where I could do ministry.

And with that revelation, I understood; my assignment was up.

"When is this supposed to happen?" I asked.

"When you're ready to partner with me, then give your resignation letter." He said.

I sat in His presence. And all I could think about was *I was being released.* And the tears rolled down my face as I realized my time had finally come. As He continued to minister to me, He made it clear that my resignation wasn't any different than any other job.

When I was ready to work for Him, give my resignation letter. In other words, the decision was mine; when I was ready. And He made it clear that He would not be the One to tell me when; I would be the one to decide. And *whenever* I decided, *that* would be the date.

Then I realized the word of the Lord was about to come to pass as I was reminded of the prophetic word that Randolph ministered in the beginning, **"By the time you finish the book, you won't even** *be at that job."* At this point, the book was in its final stages of editing.

I shared the information with Randolph. However, the Lord had already ministered the same thing to him: this decision wasn't going to come from the job and it wasn't going to come from the Lord, I had to decide. Whenever I was ready, I had to be the one to say so. So Randolph and I were in agreement with what the Lord was doing in my life.

And as far as we were concerned, there wasn't anything else that had to be said.

I was ready.

Now, in the mean time, I had decided that I was going to give my notice so that it would line up with the end of the year, which was in a few weeks. So that way, I'd start the New Year off working for the Lord, and working towards my destiny. So my mind was made up; *December 31, 2013.* I knew in my heart of hearts that the time had come for me to move on, cut my ties with that job, and do what the Lord had called me to do – full-time ministry. The Lord had finally answered my prayer.

And as if I needed a little encouragement that it was God who was instructing me, and moving on our behalf, Randolph was advised that the bonus program on his job was being discontinued.

Therefore, management was going to calculate the highest possible amount that he could have received had the program remained in place. Immediately, Randolph and I tried to calculate the amount that he could possibly get based on the $1,200 amount that he had been receiving quarterly. And let me tell you, we were happy to get that. I mean, they could've just discontinued the program and that would've been the end of it. But God!

We were astounded when he was given an increase of $10,000.00. Not just a one-time bonus, but his annual salary increased by $10,000.00! And even so, I'm sure you probably know that devil wasn't going to just let me leave the job, right? What was being said in heaven was being declared in the earth. Now, as I waited for the time to wind down to give my resignation letter, little did I know that my faith would be tested.

PROPERTY TAX BILL

All it took was that one day of balancing the checkbook, and before I knew anything, I was in warfare. "Well, you don't have to be locked into **DECEMBER 31** for your last day of work. If you need to move the date, you can," the enemy said.

"Why would I need to move the date?" I asked.

"If you need to move the date for whatever reason, you can," he said again.

"No. I'm set on that date. That's my last day." I declared.

"Well, how do you think you're going to pay the property taxes?"

"I don't know! And I don't care! I don't care about that house. If we lose the house because we couldn't pay the property taxes then so be it! I can't stay on that job! That's not where the Lord would have me!"

I mean the warfare was released in that place! Immediately, I could feel the pressure of having to pay the property taxes and we didn't have the money. But I didn't care! I was done! There was absolutely no way that I could stay on that job! It was over! It was time for me to do what God had called me to do, period!

"You're saying that, but looking at the balance in your checkbook you're not going to be able to pay the property taxes when the bill comes in." He assured me.

"I don't care if the taxes get paid or not! I believe the Lord told me that when I was ready to work for Him, give my resignation letter. And *my husband* said prophetically that 'By the time I finished the book, I wouldn't be working on that job.'" I reminded him. "You're worried about a balance and the Lord is getting ready to bless me! I don't care about those taxes!"

"Okay. You're right," he relented.

I mean that devil went in on me. It was so devastating that all I could do was sit there and cry when he left. I couldn't even get up off the couch because I was so devastated. But I wasn't about to be moved. I was done!

Now let me say this, one thing for sure that you can count on is the enemy is not going to let you "do what God called you to do" because you *believe* "God said so." You are going to be challenged; your faith is going to be tested. Therefore, you have to be prepared to, as the book of James says, submit to God, resist the devil, and he'll flee from you.

Submit yourselves therefore to God. Resist the devil, and he will flee from you.

James 4:7 KJV

And of course, I couldn't help but be reminded of Jesus in the wilderness, tempted by Satan:

Then Jesus, full of the Holy Spirit, returned from the Jordan River. He was led by the Spirit in the wilderness,

where he was tempted by the devil for forty days. Jesus ate nothing all that time and became very hungry.

Then the devil said to him, "If you are the Son of God, tell this stone to become a loaf of bread."

But Jesus told him, "No! The Scriptures say, 'People do not live by bread alone.'"

Then the devil took him up and revealed to him all the kingdoms of the world in a moment of time. "I will give you the glory of these kingdoms and authority over them," the devil said, "because they are mine to give to anyone I please.

I will give it all to you if you will worship me."

Jesus replied, "The Scriptures say, 'You must worship the Lord your God and serve only him.'"

Then the devil took him to Jerusalem, to the highest point of the Temple, and said, "If you are the Son of God, jump off!

For the Scriptures say,
'He will order his angels to protect and guard you.

And they will hold you up with their hands
so you won't even hurt your foot on a stone.'"

Jesus responded, "The Scriptures also say, 'You
must not test the Lord your God.'"

When the devil had finished tempting Jesus, he
left him until the next opportunity came.

Luke 4:1 – 13 NLT

I don't want you to be fooled into thinking that the enemy is going to stop testing you just because you were able to withstand the initial test. When the enemy saw that he couldn't get Jesus to doubt, he left him. However, keep in mind that he didn't just leave and that was the end of the temptation. No, he left *until the next opportunity came.*

What "next opportunity," you ask?

The next opportunity the enemy sees to test Him. The next opportunity the enemy sees to test you. The next opportunity when the enemy knows you're probably weak, tired, and more than likely you'll give in to the temptation.

The next opportunity when the trial gets more difficult, and you're not sure if you can go on.

The next opportunity when you think you can't hold on any longer and *want* to give up.

The next opportunity when your faith starts to waver, then you'll be defeated.

Therefore, you must understand that until you've accomplished what the Lord has purposed for you to accomplish, the enemy will continue to test you. This is his way of getting you to doubt what God has called you to do; be it full-time ministry or otherwise. It's certain to say that every step of the way you're going to be tested.

Dear brothers and sisters, when troubles of any kind come your way, consider it an opportunity for great joy.

For you know that when your faith is tested, your endurance has a chance to grow.

So let it grow, for when your endurance is fully developed, you will be perfect and complete, needing nothing.

James 1:2 – 4 NLT

And just when I thought I had it all figured out.

"What's your plan for the book?" the enemy asked.

"*I* don't have a plan."

"You *have* to have a plan. You're leaving your job and you don't have a plan?"

"I *believe* the Lord has revealed to me that my assignment is over. Therefore, I *believe* He's going to show me what to do, when to do it, and how to do it. But as far as having a plan – I don't have a plan."

"Shouldn't you be doing research in order to get a plan? Oh, you're only going to sell a few books here and a few books there, you won't be successful. But you're leaving your job, right?"

I sat there just listening. It was clear that the enemy had come yet again; therefore, I contemplated if I wanted to "go there" with him. So, I hesitated to respond. "I know I should be doing research." I said calmly. "But I'm not concerned about that. I'm not concerned about having a plan. I'm not concerned about selling any books."

I wasn't getting ready to let that devil deter me from what I knew the Lord was calling me to do. "We've gone over this before and nothing has changed since we last discussed this. I didn't know what to do *then* and I still don't know what to do *now. Nothing has changed.*"

"Well, should you be leaving your job and you don't have a plan?"

"Yes, I should. Not having a plan to sell my books has nothing to do with the Lord telling me that I had been released from my job. I trust that the Lord is going to show me what to do to sell and promote my book. As long as I'm obedient to his word, resign from the job, I'll receive the blessings He has in store for me."

It was by faith that Abraham obeyed when God called him to leave home and go to another land that God would give him as his inheritance. He went without knowing where he was going.

Hebrews 11:8 NLT

However, this time, I got up and walked away. And while the warfare had been heavy, I refused to allow it to devastate me. So I walked away to end the conversation. And just as I had expected – that devil had turned the heat up! He was not going to relent.

However, I'd like to turn your attention to the real issue here. Just as the enemy had tempted Jesus with *worldly* things, he had done the same with me: a property tax bill, a plan, a book. These things do not weigh heavily in the grand scheme of things: my destiny. But I understood the *real* test was not about a tax bill, a book, a plan, or me leaving the job.

The *real* test was to *prove* that I believed God; the *real* test was to *prove* that I believed I was partnering with God, to do full-time ministry; the *real* test was to *prove* that I believed I have been *called* by God. That's what the test was *really* about, and to see if my loyalty, my faith was divided between God and the things of the world. I believed God.

As I sat contemplating how this was all going to play out, I have to admit, I became a little emotional. This was the beginning of the end. Time was winding down. Not only was I about to close one chapter of the book, but I was about to start a new chapter. And with that being said, each day that I was on that job became that much more difficult to be there. It was difficult to come, and difficult to stay.

I was driving to work on the day I decided to give my resignation letter. I was having praise and worship in the car when the Lord showed me a vision:

In the vision...

I saw a shackle on my foot.

I submit to you today that while I can't say if I've ever had a shackle on my foot, I know for certain I had never *seen* a shackle on my foot. But immediately, I understood the enemy was trying to keep me from giving my resignation letter, and it had nothing to do with the job. The shackle was to keep me from preaching the Gospel of Jesus Christ.

I am in chains now, still preaching this message as God's ambassador.

Ephesians 6:20 NLT

But undeterred, I prayed all the more. I started to war against the enemy, binding and loosing; commanding the enemy to remove the shackle that was on my foot. Although I was bound, in chains, I was neither discouraged nor defeated; I was going to give that letter of resignation.

I was going into full-time ministry to preach the Gospel of Jesus Christ. So I started binding the hand of the enemy and loosed the Holy Spirit as I pleaded and applied the blood of Jesus to the shackle so that it would be loosed. When I applied the blood of Jesus to the shackle, *immediately,* it popped open and fell off my foot.

By the time I made it to work, it was crazy. It seemed like everything was happening. Confusion was everywhere. All kinds of distractions were going on. It was crazy. I sat at my desk trying to get my thoughts together, so I could give my letter of resignation. All of a sudden I couldn't think. So immediately, I thought *I better go get my friend to pray with me.* Demonic forces were everywhere. But when I got up to go get her, I couldn't seem to make it down there where she was. Then I knew I had to just do it. If I didn't do it right then and there, the demonic activity would only get worse. So, I went to my manager and asked if I could speak with him.

"Sure," he said unsuspectingly.

"In the office," I managed.

"Sure."

And I got the resignation letter and followed him into the office. And as soon as I sat down, I gave him the notice – effective December 31, 2013; it would be my last day of work. Whew! I did it! And immediately, the weight seemed to fall from my shoulders. I was free. It was over! I made a declaration that I wanted to partner with the Lord. And in two weeks that day would come.

Anyway, there was no turning back. THAT WAS IT! And the days went by and finally the last day had come. And with that chapter in my life being done, I turned the page.

I submit to you today that if we want to get what we've never had, then we've got to do what we've never done.

So I gave my job back to the Lord; I sowed it into the Kingdom.

One day as Jesus was walking along the shore of the Sea of Galilee, he saw two brothers—Simon, also called Peter, and Andrew—throwing a net into the water, for they fished for a living.

Jesus called out to them, "Come, follow me, and I will show you how to fish for people!"

And they left their nets at once and followed him.

Matthew 4:18 – 20 NLT

It had been six months since I quit my job. As we prepared ourselves for ministry, we knew the time was coming for my husband, Randolph, to leave his job. And suddenly, the time was upon us. As the Lord's prompting was heavy in his spirit he said, "I think it's time." And he started to plan when would be the best time to give his notice. So he decided that he'd take his vacation, mull it over, and then give his notice.

Then the Lord asked, "What are you waiting for?"

So, right then and there he decided that he would give his notice, that day. He went to work, and gave them his two-week notice. And while Randolph had anticipated working the next two weeks to fulfill his obligation of resigning, the Lord had other plans. The notice was ***effective immediately*** – the company paid him through the fifteenth of the month (even though he didn't have to go to work). They also paid him for his two weeks of vacation that he had. (The Lord wasn't playing; He wanted Randolph off that job.) So, we found ourselves with no jobs, which meant absolutely no income.

Solely; wholly trusting the Lord. And our only focus became working for the ministry; trying to get it up and running.

I will test them to see if they will follow my instructions….

Let The House Go

I can't help but be reminded of how God so graciously blessed us with our house. At the time, we lived in Schaumburg, Illinois (north suburb of Chicago). And the house we were living in had become too small for us. The kids were growing up and we needed more space. Then one day, the Lord said, "It's time to move." And immediately, I got excited and started to pack. I mean every room in the house was packed.

And day by day the boxes filled the basement, stacked one by one up against the wall in preparation of moving. I waited with expectation. And before I knew anything – a year had passed before we started looking for a house. But it was during *that* time, that we felt lead by the Spirit to move to Hazel Crest, Illinois (the south suburb of Chicago).

I can't even begin to tell you how "disappointing" that was. Randolph and I had decided that we did not want to, and would not *ever* move to the south side of Chicago. However, by the prompting of the Holy Spirit, that's exactly where He led us. In our search for a house, we were looking on the internet for homes for sale. And I have to say, *as soon as we saw the house,* we knew *it was the house* the Lord wanted us to have. We sat there almost in disbelief. I can't tell you how many times we went over the information about the house because we couldn't believe our eyes; that it was the house the Lord wanted us to have.

We called a realtor in the Hazel Crest area, and made the appointment to go see the house. Words could not express how excited we were. Immediately, we told the realtor that we knew exactly which house we wanted to see and shared the information that we had with her.

However, she wasn't able to find the house because the house wasn't listed; it was for sale by the owner. Somehow, someway, as we were riding around in the neighborhood, we saw the house. And immediately, we got excited. We knew, without a shadow of a doubt *that was the house for us.* It was almost as if it sat on a hill. It stood out from all of the houses on the block. It was white with light blue/grayish shutters that framed all of the windows. And, as it turned out, it was the biggest house on the block.

Somehow or another we had gotten the information and called the owner. We went to see the house and my God, it exceeded our expectations and still, we could not believe that this was the house the Lord was giving us. Therefore, we dedicated the house to the Lord and declared that it belonged to the Lord.

The house was a split-level home; it had four bedrooms, (three bedrooms on one side of the house for the kids and the fourth bedroom on the other side of the house for us). The kitchen was amazing; huge, white everything with a hint of blue, double oven, dishwasher, refrigerator, garbage disposal, pull-out cabinets. It had a formal dining room. It had two full baths; one upstairs and one on the lower level. The lower level was finished (and had extra space for an office). Complete area for the laundry. The lady that lived there was an interior designer, so it was absolutely beautiful. The only drawback; it had a one-car garage.

We moved into the house and quickly made it our home. Our two oldest children graduated from the high school in the Hazel Crest area. But by the time our youngest son had graduated from junior high, the Lord had called us to move to Orlando, Florida. Now it had been seven years that we'd been living in Florida, and we still had the house. And we were mindful that God so graciously made a way for us to still have the house – even through the economy collapsing and hundreds of thousands, millions of people losing their homes. The Lord made sure we were able to make *each and every payment; we never missed a single mortgage payment.*

In spite of the economy collapsing; in spite of Randolph losing his job; in spite of us being upside down on the house's value; in spite of us not being able to make the credit card payments; in spite of having to sell the Mercedes Benz; in spite of us moving to Orlando, Florida with no money, no jobs, no family, and no friends, *every single mortgage payment* was made on that house!

Well, it had been a year since I worked; we lived off of the "Joseph Funds" that we had saved up. Then we received a notice that the tenant was moving out of the house. And we were trying to decide if, and when, we were going to go to Chicago to try to find another tenant.

One thing was sure; *we* didn't have the money to pay the mortgage. But we had already determined that we weren't going to "worry" about how the mortgage was going to get paid. In fact, we had really grown tired of the house. Not to mention trying to manage the house from Florida was difficult. But in spite of it being difficult to manage, we held on to the house because we didn't know if the Lord was going to lead us back to Chicago.

Over the years we contemplated selling the house because it was difficult to manage. But that wasn't an option for me. And to be honest, I didn't want to sell the house because it somewhat gave me hope that we would go back. So I held on.

Then the Lord said, "Let the house go."

For years, we wondered if there would be a chance that we'd go back to Chicago, but after seven years in Orlando, we felt pretty confident that we wouldn't be going back. And as we had always declared, this was the Lord's house and if He said that it was time to give it up, then we were going to give up the house. We had peace concerning what the Lord was telling us to do. So, the decision had been made. We were going to let the house go. So when the tenant moved out, we would let the house go.

Now, I have to say, it baffled me that the Lord would bring us through some of the toughest times that we'd ever seen – that America has ever seen; the attack on 9/11 and the economy crashing – to *now* say, "Let the house go." And even as I sat wondering about this, I knew it was so that He'd get the glory. The Lord gets the glory when we're obedient to His commands. And because of our obedience, I believe we are on the brink of the biggest blessing we'd ever had! We were about to enter into Canaan! And I was still standing on his word…in eleven days!

So, we were ready to "let it go." We reached out to the mortgage company to advise them that we were no longer in position financially to pay the mortgage; therefore, we wanted to know what we had to do to be "released" from the mortgage; to walk away. And in the meantime, while we were trying to *figure things out* with the tenant, who was now giving us a hard time about moving out, I had a dream:

In a dream…

I was going through a door. And as I was going through the door, it started to close. I tried to stop the door from closing, but I couldn't.

The interpretation of the dream…

Immediately, I understood *the Lord* was closing the door.

What he opens, no one can close;
and what he closes, no one can open:

Revelation 3:7 NLT

There was no way that I could stop *Him* from closing the door. I was reminded of the weight of the door; it was so heavy, it felt like, and reminded me of, a vault door in a bank. I knew I couldn't stop the door from closing. In other words, the "window of opportunity;" the time in which we had *the Lord's favor* to do what He was telling us to do was about to come to an end. Therefore, it was crucial that we did what the Lord was telling us to do, "let it go." Needless to say, it's important that we do things when the Lord tells us to do them; in His timing, in order for us to receive the blessings that He has for us – in spite of the seeming obstacle with the tenant.

And consequently, we let it go; we walked away.

We believe God!

<u>When everything was ready,</u> the LORD said to Noah, "Go into the boat with all your family, for among all the people of the earth, I can see that you alone are righteous.

<u>Seven days from now</u> I will make the rains pour down on the earth. And it will rain for forty days and forty nights, until I have wiped from the earth all the living things I have created."

So Noah did everything as the LORD commanded him.

Then the LORD closed the door...

Genesis 7:1, 4 – 5; 16b NLT (emphasis added)

When it was time, the Lord gave Noah instructions to go into the boat because He was getting ready to do something; "a work" in the earth. Now it's not always for us to know what the Lord is doing or how He's going to do it. Our only responsibility is to be obedient to what He tells us to do. Nor is it our responsibility to worry about the details of how He's going to get it done. So often we find ourselves worrying about things that we have no control over. And that's usually because we aren't obedient to what He's telling us to do – so we worry, trying to figure things out on our own.

However, what we fail to realize is, when we do it in God's timing; when we do what He tells us to do, when He tells us to do it – it's easy. We don't have to worry. God will take care of the details. All we have to do is focus on what the Lord is telling us to do, and do that!

The Lord told Noah that in **seven days** He was going to make it rain. So, Noah had seven days to complete what the Lord was telling Him to do. Seven days – was His "window of opportunity." If he missed the seven day window, he would miss the blessing of what the Lord was doing; saving him and his family (and the animals).

Noah did everything as the LORD commanded him.

Then the LORD closed the door.

It was by faith that Noah built a large boat to save his family from the flood. He obeyed God, who warned him about things that had never happened before.

Hebrews 11:7 NLT

I couldn't help but notice, *who warned him about things that had never happened before.* In other words, the Lord warned Noah of what was to come; the impending danger. The Lord knew what was getting ready to happen and He was closing the door to keep Noah from being defeated. I said that to say this, you don't want the door to close before you do what the Lord told you to do; or else you'll be swept away. You will be overtaken. You'll miss the "window of opportunity." You'll miss the blessings of what God is doing in your life.

God wants to know if He can trust us. He wants to know if you're going to be obedient. I have to admit, I couldn't seem to figure out why the tenant wouldn't just move out. She said she had a place, she wasn't living in our house, and yet she was giving us a hard time about leaving. It didn't make sense to me.

I couldn't help but be reminded of Pharaoh. How, in spite of Moses telling Pharaoh to let the people of God go, the Lord hardened Pharaoh's heart, so that Pharaoh wouldn't let the people go. Ultimately, it was so that God would get the glory out of what He was doing for His people. Somehow, someway I knew God was going to get the glory out of this situation. But I couldn't help but think, somehow, someway, He was hardening the heart of the tenant; causing her not to leave, so that *we* would trust Him in this process; so that *we* would be obedient, and He would get the glory in the end.

Then the Lord responded:

One morning after Randolph and I finished praying, a spirit of praise came upon me. And as I praised the Lord, the vision was before me:

In the vision...

I saw myself giving birth. And as the baby was coming forth, I noticed the baby was breech. He was being delivered feet first. As the baby came forth, seemingly, the head was stuck. Then, the hand of God reached in and delivered the head – delivering the baby.

The interpretation of the vision...

It looks like things are not going right. It looks like this is not the way the baby should come; this is not the way to deliver a baby. But the Lord is saying, "He's going to deliver the baby. He's going to make it happen."

While it looks like you're stuck. And it looks like what God promised is not going to happen, or it looks like it's going to be difficult – God is going to do it. It looks like you're not going to be able to accomplish what the Lord said you'd accomplish, He's going to do it! He's going to make it happen!

And He's going to get the glory!

It looked like we were stuck because the tenant was giving us a hard time about moving out. It looked like we weren't going to be able to get the approval from the mortgage company. It looked like we were just going to have to walk away.

But God said, "He's going to deliver this thing!"

I couldn't help but think about the birthing process as God births this thing in our lives: While most babies shift or turn head-first into the birthing canal; into the delivery position, there are some babies who do not. And when they don't turn, they're considered to be in a breech position. Being in a breech position means the baby is positioned to come either buttock-first or feet-first.

In the vision, as I mentioned, the baby was in what is called the footling breech position; he was being delivered by both feet coming out first. Now here is what the Lord said, "It's not going to happen the way you think it's going to happen." And with that being said, I must confess: I thought we were going to reach out to the mortgage company, the tenant would move out, and it would be a wrap. But that's far from what happened. The Lord said, "I'm not going to turn this one around." *(He's going to deliver it breech.)* And He's going to get the glory!

Sometimes the baby doesn't turn because they don't have enough room in the uterus to turn. Then, I couldn't help but wonder, *are we allowing God enough room to birth the things in our lives; to work miracles in our lives?* He's not going to turn this one around. What seems to be impossible with man is possible with God.

It may not look like things are going to work out. It may not look like things are okay. But God is going to deliver this one! Initially, the thing that I struggled with was the fact that this woman is in *my* house and there was nothing I could do about it. *This* was different than when I walked away after owing the credit card companies; *this time,* somebody owed me! But *I* had to walk away. I struggled with that!

But in spite of my struggle, I continued to give the situation to the Lord. I continued to declare and decree that "we had been released from the mortgage." However, I found myself "waiting" to see what the Lord was going to do. I was "waiting" to see how it was all going to end. In essence, I was *"waiting"* on the Lord. Then one day the Lord said, "You aren't 'waiting' to be released, you are already released!"

And suddenly, as the tears began to fall from my eyes, I understood that while I had been focused on what the tenant had been doing, and the problems that she was giving us, the Lord was focusing on me; highlighting the fact that the issue wasn't with the tenant. The issue was with *me* – did I believe He was going to do this? Did I believe He was able to do this?

I wasn't waiting on the Lord. I wasn't waiting on the mortgage company. I wasn't waiting on the tenant. It was already done! And yet, I was still holding on...*waiting*. It was already done! I didn't have to *wait* to see what was going to happen – it had already happened.

So I let go; I walked away!

GOD CLOSED THAT DOOR!

These are the words of him who is holy and true, who holds the key of David. What he opens no one can shut, and what he shuts no one can open.

Revelation 3:7 NIV

Epilogue
Do Whatever He Tells You

In my spirit I kept hearing, "Get out of debt." *Financial freedom* continued to ring out in my spirit as I anticipated the blessings of the Lord in my own life, my own situation. I was excited about how the Lord was getting ready to get us out of debt!

And while I've shared with you how the Lord has brought me out of debt, how He delivered me from the bondage of debt, how He released me from the obligation of debt, I understand that the way that He took *me through* may not necessarily be the way that He'll take *you through;* and lead you out of debt.

Therefore, I would like to make it clear, that I am not telling you to do everything that the Lord told me to do, but I *am* telling you to, *"Do whatever He tells you"* in order to become debt free! Often times, in order for us to become financially free, it requires:

- ❖ Some to give.
- ❖ Some to tithe.
- ❖ Some to let go!

And only the Lord will determine which *you'll* need to do.

The next day there was a wedding celebration in the village of Cana in Galilee. Jesus' mother was there,

and Jesus and his disciples were also invited to the celebration.

The wine supply ran out during the festivities, so Jesus' mother told him, "They have no more wine."

"Dear woman, that's not our problem," Jesus replied. "My time has not yet come."

But his mother told the servants, "Do whatever he tells you."

Standing nearby were six stone water jars, used for Jewish ceremonial washing. Each could hold twenty to thirty gallons.

Jesus told the servants, "Fill the jars with water." When the jars had been filled,

he said, "Now dip some out, and take it to the master of ceremonies." So the servants followed his instructions.

When the master of ceremonies tasted the water that was now wine, not knowing where it had

come from (though, of course, the servants knew),
he called the bridegroom over.

"A host always serves the best wine first," he said.
"Then, when everyone has had a lot to drink, he
brings out the less expensive wine. But you have
kept the best until now!"

This miraculous sign at Cana in Galilee was the
first time Jesus revealed his glory. And his
disciples believed in him.

John 2:1 – 11 NLT

You're probably already familiar with Jesus' first miracle; turning water into wine. However, there are a few things that I'd like to point out that the Lord revealed to me concerning this passage of scriptures and you becoming debt free. Let's take a look:

But His mother told the servants, "Do whatever
He tells you."

John 2:5 NLT

Manna is in verse two:

[and Jesus and his disciples were also invited to the
celebration.]

Bread from Heaven: Jesus was *invited* to the wedding celebration. So the first thing I want to suggest to you towards getting out of debt, the first thing I want to suggest to you towards your financial freedom; the first thing I want to suggest to you towards you being released from your financial obligations is:

❖ *You have to invite Jesus into your situation.*

Of course He knows that you're struggling, and He knows about everything that you're going through. He knows about all of the pain and suffering that you're enduring as a result of being in debt. He sees all of the tears and the frustration. He knows how difficult it is for you to have to decide between paying a bill and eating. He knows about all of your concerns, worry, and anxiety. He knows you're robbing Peter to pay Paul.

In fact, you're robbing Peter to pay Paul; then you rob Paul to pay Peter! He is very much aware of everything that's going on with you. However, He's not going to intervene in your situation until you first *invite* Him in to intervene. He's not going to intervene in your situation until, that is, you *give* your situation to Him; He's not going to intervene in your situation until you *trust* Him to fix it for you; He's not going to intervene in your situation until you *believe* He can fix it for you.

When you've done all that you can do; when you can't see your way out; when you come to the end of your rope; when you're sick and tired of being sick and tired, *invite Jesus into your situation.*

Manna is in verse three:

[The wine supply ran out during the festivities,]

Bread from Heaven: You have to come to the realization that you don't have the resources. Now, we all know, and I think it's safe to say, that running out of wine at your wedding would be very embarrassing. But aside from the embarrassment, the focus and the fact remain: the wine supply ran out.

And I'm sure many of you have found that while you haven't *run out of wine,* you've run out of finances. You have nothing left! And you can't see your way out of your situation. You've gotten in over your head. You're drowning in debt. You've bitten off more than you can chew. You're down to nothing. How embarrassing!

❖ *You have to come to the realization that you have nothing left*

Well, first of all, let me encourage you: When you're down to nothing, God is up to something! So let us take our eyes off of the situation, and put our eyes on God, and allow Him to work things out. We don't know *what* He's going to do, but we know He *can* do it! If you don't see your situation as a problem; if you think there's nothing wrong with the way you live; if you think there's nothing wrong with the way you manage your finances; if you think robbing Peter to Paul is acceptable; if you think that going from paycheck to paycheck (scared to miss a check) is an acceptable standard of living, then – *that's* a problem.

In order for you to get on the road to becoming debt free, you have to come to the realization that you don't have the resources to maintain the lifestyle that you've become accustomed to, which usually means you're living above your means.

If you have more month left at the end of the month than you have money, then you have to come to the realization that *you have nothing left*.

More ***Manna*** is in verse three:

> *[so Jesus' mother told him, "They have no more wine."]*

Bread from Heaven: You have to tell Jesus your problem. Mary points out to Jesus what *seems* to be an obvious problem. On the surface we know there isn't any more wine; however, we don't see the *root cause* of this situation. Yes, it could've been a simple mistake; miscalculating the amount needed versus the number of people that would be attending. And the same could very well hold true for you. And I understand that this may be a little more difficult than what appears on the surface, but we need to get to the *root* of *why* you have this problem.

❖ *You have to tell Jesus your problem.*

We've miscalculated the amount of income we had coming in versus the debts we've accumulated. It could've very well been as a result of the economy crashing, you lost your job or whatever the case may have been. But what I'd like to share with you today is that what may not be as obvious is that which is *below the surface;* and that is the fact that we've placed our trust, our dependence in the world's system instead of in Jesus. We've trusted in jobs, houses, cars, clothes.

Instead of renewing our minds, instead of living for the Kingdom of God, we've tried to make a living on our own via the world's system. We only trust what the world has taught us. We live by the principles that we've been raised on, and we've duplicated the same financial indebtedness in our families that were in our parents' family, and their parents' family. We don't live by Kingdom principles (more so, because we don't know what those principles are.) But God is trying to lead us out of Egypt to take us into the Promised Land. God is trying to get us to trust Him with our finances.

Manna is in verse four:

["Why have you involved me?"]

Bread from Heaven: You have to put your trust in Him. Every time we see someone in the bible that has a need, they approach Jesus with that need; they come to Him. And often times, He'll challenge the person and ask *why* they think He can meet their need. However, it doesn't by anyway mean that He's not going to help; the question is rhetorical.

It's *really* an opportunity for you to look at your situation; look at where you are...spiritually. It's really just an opportunity for *you* to see where your faith is. Do you *really* believe He can do this? Do you *really* trust that He'll do it? Are you *really* walking by faith? His question is the same as when you ask someone to loan you, let's say, $100.00. And they say, "What makes you think I have $100.00?" And usually you'll say *why* you think the person has the money; "Because I *know*..." Then they usually end up giving you the money.

Well, the same holds true for the Lord. He wants to know do you *know* Him? Do you *know* what He's capable of doing? Do you **kno**w that He can change your situation?

❖ *You have to put your trust in Him.*

Not only is He challenging your faith, but it's also an opportunity for you to tell Him what it is that you want Him to do for you. In essence, He's asking you, ***"What do you want me to do?"***

More ***Manna*** is in verse four:

["Why have you involved me?"]

Bread from Heaven: You have to tell Him what you want Him to do for you. I'm reminded of blind Bartimaeus.

Then they came to Jericho. As Jesus and his disciples, together with a large crowd, wee leaving the city, a blind man, Bartimaeus (which means "Son of Timaeus"), was sitting by the roadside begging.

When he heard that it was Jesus of Nazareth, he began to shout, "Jesus, Son David, have mercy on me!"

Many rebuked him and told him to be quiet, but he shouted all the more, "Son of David, have mercy on me!"

Jesus stopped and said, "Call him."

So they called to the blind man, "Cheer up! On your feet! He is calling you."

Throwing his cloak aside, he jumped to his feet and came to Jesus.

"What do you want me to do for you?" Jesus asked him.
The blind man said, "Rabbi, I want to see."

"Go," said Jesus, "your faith has healed you." Immediately he received his sight and followed Jesus along the road.

Mark 10: 46 – 52 NIV

How many times have we asked God to do something for us, but we weren't prepared to receive from Him; because we don't *know* Him. We call on God to provide for us, but we don't *know* Him as Jehovah Jireh; our Provider.

Why have *you* involved Him?

More *Manna* is in verse four:

["My hour has not yet come."]

Bread from Heaven: You have to have a revelation of who Jesus is. Jesus was saying He didn't want His *identity* revealed. He didn't want the people to *know* who He really was because the people weren't *ready* to receive Him for who He *really* was. Guess what? He hasn't revealed Himself to *us* because **we're not ready – we're not prepared.** We're looking for a miracle, but we're not prepared for the miracle. We're not prepared (spiritually) to see Him as the miracle worker. We're not developed, mature, enough spiritually to see His identity, His character as the miracle worker. We don't fully understand the *reality* of what a miracle is. This is a side of God we've never seen before:

❖ *You have to have a revelation of who Jesus is.*

We *think* we know Him, but we don't.

When he had finished speaking, he said to Simon, "Now go out where it is deeper, and let down your nets to catch some fish."

"Master," Simon replied, "we worked hard all last night and didn't catch a thing. But if you say so, I'll let the nets down again."

And this time their nets were so full of fish they began to tear!

A shout for help brought their partners in the other boat, and soon both boats were filled with fish and on the verge of sinking.

__When Simon Peter realized what had happened, he fell to his knees before Jesus and said, "Oh, Lord, please leave me—I'm too much of a sinner to be around you."__

__For he was awestruck by the number of fish they had caught, as were the others with him.__

Luke 5:4 – 9 NLT (emphasis added)

Peter had a revelation of who Jesus was. Although Peter had seen Jesus perform other miracles: cast out demons and heal the sick, he hadn't had a *personal encounter* with Jesus. But this time, Jesus provided what **Peter** needed. And when Peter realized *that,* he came to know Jesus on a *personal* level. He **knew** Him for himself. Not because he saw what Jesus had done for other people, but because of what Jesus had done for *him!*

Allow me to explain it this way: Back in 2007 when all of this started, the beginning of our financial downfall that is, we could've called the mortgage company *then* and said to them that we wanted to be released from our mortgage, right? Well, not really because in 2007 that's not what we wanted. Besides, I didn't have the *mindset* of living according to Kingdom principles – back then.

We were still living in, and depending on, the world's system, so my mind hadn't been renewed to see and trust the Lord to deliver me out of Egypt. So in essence, what I'm saying is, it wasn't *His time to reveal Himself* to me because I wasn't ready to **receive** and **trust** Him on *that* level; as the miracle worker.

It wasn't time for the Lord to deliver me – it wasn't time for Him to perform a miracle because I wasn't capable; ready to receive it. I wasn't mature enough spiritually to see and understand what the Lord was doing. So, **then** wasn't the time for Him to reveal His identity to me.

Manna is in verse five:

[But his mother told the servants, "Do whatever He tells you."]

Bread from Heaven: You have to do whatever He tells you. Mary wanted Jesus to do something. She may not have known *what* He was going to do or *how* He was going to do it, but she *knew* He *would* do something!

Whenever we find ourselves in a position where we've done all that we can do, more often than not, we know to call on Jesus to help us. But more often than not, we're not willing to do what He tells us to do. And because we've put our trust in the "things" that we've acquired, "things" that have given us a false sense of security, "things" that have given us a false sense of identity, it's difficult to let these "things" go. It's difficult to walk away from them.

But in order for you to allow Jesus to lead you out of Egypt; out of financial bondage,

"Do whatever He tells you."

Like Mary, I may not know *what* He's going to do or *how* He's going to do it, but I do *know* He's going to *do* something! Now, whether he tells you:

- ❖ Stop "robbing Peter to pay Paul" – Stop putting your trust in credit cards
- ❖ Sell your car (or give it back to the lender)
- ❖ Sell your house (or give it back to the lender)
- ❖ Leave your home town and go to the land I'll show you
- ❖ Sow a seed
- ❖ Start tithing
- ❖ Let go!

Do whatever He tells you!

God would not have us to suffer; financially or otherwise. He would not have us to live in financial bondage. He would not have us to live paycheck to paycheck!

He wants us to live the abundant life that He came to give us.

The thief's purpose is to steal and kill and destroy. My purpose is to give them a rich and satisfying life."

John 10:10 NLT

In order to achieve financial freedom; in order to become debt free, we must be *willing* to do *whatever* He tells us to do. We must be obedient to what He tells us to do. *He has come to lead us out of Egypt; lead us out of bondage.* So we may live the abundant; rich and satisfying life.

More *Manna* is in verse five:

[But his mother told the servants, "Do whatever He tells you."]

Bread from Heaven: You have to trust His timing. Do whatever He tells you; **whenever** He tells you. Mary wanted Him to do something. And she trusted His timing – it's done in His timing!

"Therefore, say to the Israelite: 'I am the LORD, and I will bring you out from under the yoke of the Egyptians. I will free you from being slaves to

them, and I will redeem you with an outstretched arm and with mighty acts of judgment.

I will take you as my own people, and I will be your God. Then you will know that I am the LORD your God, who brought you out from under the yoke of the Egyptians.

And I will bring you to the land I swore with uplifted hand to give to Abraham, to Isaac and to Jacob. I will give it to you as a possession. I am the LORD.'"

Exodus 6:6 – 8 NIV (emphasis added)

We don't *trust* the Lord because we don't *know* the LORD. God was getting ready to use Moses to reveal Himself to the people so that they would come to know Him as "the LORD." To establish a ***personal relationship*** with the people; to reveal a new understanding of God's character – a closer identification between God and His people.

He was getting ready to start a personal relationship with Israel; His divine presence would fulfill the promises made to Abraham, Isaac and Jacob. And the same holds true for us. God is ready to deliver us; He's ready to reveal Himself, His identity, character. He's ready to show us who He is, so that we may get a revelation, a personal relationship with Him. NOW is the time to trust Him to do just what He said He'd do. NOW is the time to get to **know** Him. NOW is the time for you to do whatever He tells you to do.

We see that the world's system doesn't work. We saw when the economy crashed there was absolutely no help for the people, but the people who, in essence, caused the crash were the very ones who received the help! This is evidence that only the Lord will take care of us!

Manna is in verse six:

[Standing nearby were six stone water jars, used for Jewish ceremonial washing. Each could hold twenty to thirty gallons.]

Bread from Heaven: You have to expect your miracle. We know *nearby* means near; close at hand. And *each* means every one of two or more considered separately. And all I have to say about that is: *your miracle is nearby! Your answer is nearby! Your promise is nearby! And each one is going to be huge! Each one is going to be abundant! Each one is going to bless you beyond measure!*

❖ You have to expect your miracle.

You have to confidently expect; walk by faith and not by sight; you have to believe the Lord is going to do just what He said He would do! When it looks like nothing is going to happen, you have to expect God to do the impossible! When it feels like it's not going to happen, you have to believe – against all odds, God's going to do it! When you get tired of waiting for it to come to pass, you have to hold on! When it seems like it's not possible, trust Him! Walk by faith!

Manna is in verse seven:

[Jesus told the servants, "Fill the jars with water."]

Bread from Heaven: You have to fill your jar with water. You may or may not understand that *water* represents the *Holy Spirit.* And it goes without saying that in order for you to receive from Jesus; in order for you to follow His instructions; *you must be filled with His Holy Spirit.* Your jar is your body; your vessel; your temple.

In order to receive from the Lord, you have to be connected to His Spirit, lead by His Spirit. To follow His instructions, to be able to do what He's telling you to do, you must have a personal relationship with Him; His Holy Spirit. It's time to take your relationship with Him to another level: prayer, fasting, praise and worship, studying the word of God, building yourself up on your most holy faith (speaking in tongues), and assembling yourself with other believers – go to church to be fed. Fill your vessel with the Holy Spirit.

❖ Fill your jar with water.

But when the Father sends the Advocate as my representative – that is, the Holy Spirit – he will teach you everything and will remind you of everything I have told you.

John 14:26 NLT

We now have this light shining in our hearts, but we ourselves are like fragile clay jars containing this great treasure.

2 Corinthians 4:7a NLT

Knowing that God uses us to spread his Good News, and he gives us power to do his work; knowing that the power is His, not ours, should keep us from pride and motivate us to keep daily contact with God, our power source. Our responsibility is to let people see God through us. And we can't do that if we're bogged down with debt; we can't do that if we're trusting more in the world's system than we trust God. And we can't do that if we're hard pressed on every side:

We are pressed on every side by troubles, but we are not crushed. We are perplexed, but not driven to despair.

We are hunted down, but never abandoned by God. We get knocked down, but we are not destroyed.

Through suffering, our bodies continue to share in the death of Jesus so that the life of Jesus may also be seen in our bodies.

2 Corinthians 4:8 – 10 NLT

We may think, and it may feel like, we're at the end of our rope, but God never abandons us.

"Don't let your hearts be troubled. Trust in God, and trust also in me."

John 14:1 NLT

Don't let your hearts be troubled. Trust in God; God would not have us to suffer.

I am leaving you with a gift – peace of mind and heart. And the peace I give is a gift the world cannot give. So don't be troubled or afraid.

John 14:27 NLT

Don't be concerned about what people will say; don't be concerned about your credit score – the

Lord will take care of that (if you're obedient to His commands). He's trying to get you from under this rock. You have gotten to this point on your own, and if you're as desperate as I was, your credit is probably already affected. While you're concerned about your "credit score," your life is falling apart. While you're trying to keep up appearances, you're family is falling apart. There is only one way to go from here; there is only one thing to do from here; trust the Lord. I thank God that your *creditability* isn't measured by a scoring system; either you trust God or you don't! Either you walk by faith or you don't! Either you're obedient to His commands or you're not!

It's as simple as that. God has given each of us *a measure of faith:*

For I say, through the grace given unto me, to every man that is among you, not to think of himself more highly than he ought to think; but to think soberly, according as God hath dealt to every man the measure of faith.

Romans 12:3 KJV

We walk by faith not by sight. We can't be concerned about what other people will say; walk by faith! We can't be concerned about our credit; walk by faith! We can't be concerned about having to get on the bus; walk by faith! We can't be concerned about living in an apartment; walk by faith! *Fill your jar, your vessel, with the Holy Spirit!*

Manna is in verse eight:

> *[He said, "Now dip some out, and take it to the master of ceremonies."]*

Bread from Heaven: You have to dip some out. Now in this case, *"some"* means *the water that had been put in the jars.* Because *that's* what the Lord was going to *use* in order to create the wine; that's what the Lord was going to *use* in order to *give* the groom what He *needed.*

❖ You have to dip some out.

But in your case, *"some"* means *the Holy Spirit* that has been put in your jars; *the faith* that has been put in your jars. Because *that's* what the Lord is going to *use* in order to create the miracle; that's what the Lord is going to *use* in order to *give* you what you *need.*

In *your* case, *"some"* is *whatever* you need more of.

Well, let me say it this way: If you, like the groom at the wedding, have run out of *something* that you need, then take *some* of what you *need* out of what you *have*. Okay, let me say it *this* way: If you need more money, take "some" out of the money you have.

Now, I know you already know what I'm about to say, but I have to say it anyway.

More **Manna** is in verse eight:

[He said, "Now dip some out, and take it to the master of ceremonies."]

Bread from Heaven: You have to take it to the Master *of ceremonies.*

There. I said it. This is what the Lord is saying, "Take 'some' of what you have and give it to the Master." If you need money, take "some" of the money you have and give it to the Master. Give it to the Master.

❖ You have to take it to the Master.

Sow a seed. Sow a seed of faith. Sow it into the kingdom of God.

Now, there is no way that I can continue without acknowledging that we don't *know* when the water *actually* turned into wine. There isn't any indication that when the water was *poured* into the jars, immediately it turned to wine. Otherwise, I think it would've been mentioned, and witnessed by the servants who were pouring the wine.

We don't *know* if the water turned into wine in the *process* of it being taken to the master; *on the way* to being given to the master. Again, there isn't any indication of that either. And again, I think it would've been mentioned, and witnessed by the servants who took the wine to the master of ceremonies.

Nor do we *know* if the water turned into wine when the servants *gave* the water to the master of ceremonies. Again, there isn't any indication of that either. And, like I said, I think it would've been mentioned, and witnessed by the servants who gave the wine to the master of ceremonies.

But we *do know* that when the master of ceremonies *tasted* the water, it was *already* wine.

I'm saying all of that to say this: We don't know *when* or *how* the miracle happened, but we *do know* it happened!

I'm saying all of that to say this: *Somewhere* in the *process* of them *filling the jars, dipping some out* and *taking it to the master* of ceremonies – the miracle happened!

I'm saying all of that to say this: When the master of ceremonies *tasted* it – the miracle had *already* happened! When the master of ceremonies *received it* – the miracle had *already* happened!

I'm saying all of that to say this: When you *receive* what the Lord is doing in your life – the miracle has *already* happened. It's *already* done! When you *receive* it!

I'm saying all of that to say this: We don't know *when* or *how* your miracle is going to happen, but we *do know* – it *will* happen! We don't know *when* or *how* your miracle is going to happen, but we *do know* that it's *in the process* of you *filling the jars, dipping some out; taking what you have, and giving it to the Master* – it *will* happen!

We don't know *when* or *how* the miracle is going to happen, but we *do know* that when the Master tastes it; when the Master receives it – *when you give it to Him,* it would've already happened!

I'm saying all of that to say this: We don't know when our seed is going to take root and bring forth the harvest; we don't know when our seed is going to take root and bring forth the miracle. We don't know if it's going to be when we fill the jars – the harvest will come. We don't know if it's going to be when we dip some out – the harvest will come. We don't know if it's going to be when we take it to the Master – the harvest will come. We don't know if it's going to be when the Master tastes it; receives it as an offering – the harvest will come.

Therefore, we have to continue to sow until the miracle manifests.

Because we don't know *which* seed that we sow is going to take root and bring forth the harvest.

More *Manna* is in verse eight:

[So the servants followed his instructions]

Bread from Heaven: You have to follow His instructions. Let me also say this, if we pour the water in the jars, and we start focusing on filling our lives with the Holy Spirit, but we don't follow His instructions – nothing will happen. If we pour water in the jars, and dip some out; if we commit to praise and worship, and make a decision that we're going to take some of what we have, but we don't follow His instructions – nothing will happen. If we pour water in the jars, if we commit to prayer, make a decision that we're going to take some of what we have, and give it to the Master, but we don't follow His instructions – nothing will happen.

If we follow His instructions – we can expect a miracle!

❖ You have to follow His instructions.

We have to be obedient to His instructions. We don't know which act of obedience is going to cause the miracle to manifest. We don't know which seed that we sow is going to cause the miracle to manifest. We don't know if the miracle happens when it leaves our hands or when it enters His mouth. They followed His instructions!

That's the absolute most important part: They followed His instructions. If Jesus gave the instructions, but they didn't do what He told them to do then there wouldn't have been a miracle. I hope you know that this isn't about turning the water into wine – This is about your miracle! Whatever miracle you need – He'll provide supernaturally!

We want a miracle; we have to get to know the miracle worker. We want a miracle; we have to do what He says do. His time to reveal Himself to you has not yet come – because you're not prepared. Jesus, completely in tune with the will of God, waits for the right moment to reveal Himself to us; to fulfill the purpose for which God had sent Him into the world.

"Therefore, be careful to obey every command I am giving you today, so you may have strength to

go in and take over the land you are about to enter.

If you obey, you will enjoy a long life in the land the LORD swore to give to your ancestors and to you, their descendants – a land flowing with milk and honey!

For the land you are about to enter and take over is not like the land of Egypt from which you came, where you planted your seed and made irrigation ditches with your foot as in a vegetable garden.

Rather, the land you will soon take over is a land of hills and valleys with plenty of rain –

a land that the LORD your God cares for. He watches over it through each season of the year!

Deuteronomy 11:8 – 12 NLT

Manna is in verse ten:

["A host always serves the best wine first," He said. "Then when everyone has had a lot to drink, he brings out the less expensive wine. But you have kept the best until now!"]

Bread from Heaven: You have to give Him praise. I think it's safe to say that we have lived what we would probably consider the best life that we could've possibly lived. We have always wanted nothing but the best and would settle for nothing less. I think it's safe to say that our decisions have been, more often than not, the best decisions we could make, at that particular time, with what we thought was our best interest in mind.

But, let us not forget, it was the "best" that *we* could provide for ourselves. It was the "best" that the *world* had to offer. But the world's best can't compare to the best that the Lord has for us!

Your best is yet to come! The Lord has saved the best for last.

> ❖ You have to give Him praise.

The Lord promises restoration:

Rejoice, you people of Jerusalem!
Rejoice in the LORD your God!
For the rain he sends demonstrates his faithfulness.
Once more the autumn rains will come,
as well as the rains of spring.

Joel 2:23 NLT

Trust Him. He will provide. His promise of restoration will be fulfilled in your life! He's going to give back everything that the enemy stole from you! You thought you lived a good life; wait until you see what God is getting ready to do NOW. Be restored! Be made whole; nothing lacking, nothing missing! Your latter rain will be greater than your former rain! Greater is coming! Praise Him!

Manna is in verse eleven:

[This miraculous sign at Cana in Galilee was the first time Jesus revealed His glory.   And His disciples believed in him.]

Bread from Heaven: You have to believe in Him. This, Jesus' first miraculous sign, was the first time Jesus revealed His glory, and His disciples believed in Him; put their faith in Him.

God's glory, the miracle is so that you'll believe. God's glory, the miracle is so that you can get to see Him in a way that you've never seen Him before. God's glory, the miracle is so that you can get to experience Him in a way that you've never experienced Him before. God's glory, the miracle is so that you can get to know Him in a way that you've never known Him before. God's glory, the miracle is for your sake! That you will believe.

Miracles are to demonstrate God's power and authority. Miracles are to demonstrate God's character, identity. Miracles are to demonstrate He is God.

"I am the true grapevine, and my Father is the gardener.

He cuts off every branch of mine that doesn't produce fruit, and he prunes the branches that do bear fruit so they will produce even more.

You have already been pruned and purified by the message I have given you.

Remain in me, and I will remain in you. For a branch cannot produce fruit if it is severed from the vine, and you cannot be fruitful unless you remain in me."

John 15:1 – 4 NLT

PROPHETIC WORD

"I see you," says the Lord. "Now come into agreement, align with your purpose, and embrace who you are in me; not what you think about yourself or what you hear others say. I have brought you into this place that you would experience me, that you would trust my plans.

There has been a shift in the spirit. I have moved you into a new place; a place that you are not familiar with.

As you speak, release prayers of hope and faith; you are prophesying to your destiny.

In this new place I am enlarging your capacity to receive of me that you would do great and mighty exploits in this season. Signs, wonders, and miracles are your portion. Where I have placed you it flows with milk and honey (wealth). This is a place of abundance, promotion, and increase. Will you trust me? With your eyes it looks like lack and inefficiency. I will give you vision to walk in purpose.

I am Jehovah- Jireh, your Provider. Your provisions are in Me," says the Spirit of Grace.

Prophet Demoine Dominguez

ABOUT DAISY S. DANIELS

Daisy S. Daniels has been married to Randolph E. Daniels, Sr. for 23 years. They have three children: Ronald, DaiSha, and Randolph, Jr. Daisy is Pastor of The Embassy of Grace (co-laborer with Senior Pastor, Randolph Daniels). She is an anointed woman of God who operates in the apostolic five-fold ministry in the body of Christ; under a prophetic mantle.

Prophetess Daisy's leadership, motivational, and transformational expertise encourages, inspires, and empowers the body of Christ.

She is founder and CEO of Daisy S. Daniels Ministries; a ministry that empowers women to increase in mind, body, soul and spirit; to break spiritual, physical, psychological, emotional, and sexual strongholds.

She is President and CEO of The Writing on the Wall Publishing Services; a full-service Christian publishing house that is committed to excellence in Christian-theme publications that enables you to write and publish the books of your dreams.

She received her M.B.A. in International Business from Keller Graduate School of Management in 2011.

TO CONTACT THE AUTHOR

Write: Daisy S. Daniels
P.O. BOX 621433
Orlando, FL 32862
Telephone: (708) 704-6117
Email: daisysdaniels@aol.com
Website:
www.daisysdaniels.wix.com/ministry

ALSO BY DAISY S. DANIELS

THE TIES THAT BIND

BIRTHING MINISTRY

21-DAY FAITH FAST

YOUR FAITH IS ON TRIAL

INCREASE!

THE WRITING ON THE WALL
PUBLISHING SERVICES

The Writing on the Wall Publishing Services is a Christian publishing house that is committed to excellence in Christian-theme publications.

The Writing on the Wall Publishing Services' goal is to equip you with the tools needed to successfully write, publish, and print your books. Our services include:

- MANUSCRIPT REVIEW
- EDITING
- MANUSCRIPT DEVELOPMENT / CONSULTING
- PAGE DESIGN AND LAYOUT
- COVER DESIGN
- ISBN NUMBER / BOOKLAND EAN BARCODE
- PRINTING
- COPYRIGHT

For more information, contact us:

Write: The Writing on the Wall Publishing Services
P.O. BOX 621433
Orlando, FL 32862 – 1433
Telephone: (708) 704-6117
Email: thewritingonthewall@aol.com
Website:
www.thewritingonthewal.wix.com/daisysdaniels